SPLENDORS OF

ISTANBUL

❖

Houses and Palaces along
the Bosporus

SPLENDORS OF
ISTANBUL

✣

Houses and Palaces along
the Bosporus

CHRIS HELLIER

Photographs by
FRANCESCO VENTURI
& CHRIS HELLIER

Abbeville Press   Publishers
New York   London   Paris

Editorial note: Because this book was published simultaneously in the United States and Great Britain, and the author is British, the conventional British spelling *Bosphorus* has been retained throughout the text.

First published in the United States of America in 1993 by Abbeville Press, 488 Madison Avenue, New York, NY 10022.

First published in Great Britain in 1993 by Tauris Parke Books, 45 Bloomsbury Square, London WC1A 2HY in association with KEA Publishing Services Ltd, London.

Text and captions © 1993 Chris Hellier
Photographs © 1993 Francesco Venturi/KEA Publishing Services Ltd and Chris Hellier

The Cataloguing in Publication Data for this book is available from the British Library.

ISBN 1-55859-600-3

FRONT JACKET One of two stone lions, brought from Egypt in 1860, which guard the quay of the mid-nineteenth-century Sait Halim Pasha yali.

BACK JACKET Ahmet III's Fruit Room, or dining room, at Topkapi Palace, built and decorated in 1706; the background shows tile panels from the Topkapi's notorious 'Prison of the Princes'.

FRONTISPIECE The eighteenth-century Zarif Mustafa Pasha yali on the Asian shore was badly damaged recently when a ship rammed its seafront façade. Impenetrable fog and strong Bosphorus currents are major navigational hazards.

FOR JOËLLE AND NAOMI

— ❖ —

ACKNOWLEDGEMENTS

I am indebted to many people for their help and hospitality during the preparation of this book. In particular I would like to thank Ömer Koç for valuable assistance in the early stages of the project, for the loan of material, and for the use of *Maviden*, a Koç family boat. I am also indebted to the owners and occupants of several featured yalis: to Mrs Mihda Bilgişin and Mr Selim Dirvana of the Kibrisli yali; to Mrs Ayşegül Nadir who is patiently restoring the Sa'dullah Pasha yali at Çengelköy; to Mrs Ruya Nebioğlu of the Mocan yali at Kuzguncuk; and to Mr Selahattin Bayazit who inherited the Çürüksulu yali at Salacak from the late Turkish diplomat Mr Nuri Birgi. While photographing the state-owned palaces and the Sherifler yali at Emirgan, as well as the Sait Halim Pasha yali owned by the Development Bank of Turkey, I was invariably met by hospitable and patient staff.

Much of the research for the book was undertaken in the 'Istanbul Library' of Dr Çelik Gülersoy. The library is one of the most valuable sources of material about the city and the friendly, efficient librarians make it a delight to use. It is also the only library I know where tea is served at readers' desks in the afternoon. I wish the library every success and thank Dr Gülersoy for information about the Egyptian villa at Çubuklu.

I would like to thank my editor at Tauris Parke Books, Judy Spours, for her valuable comments and suggestions on early drafts of the text. A special thanks also to my wife Joëlle, my best critic, for her continual support and for translating several important documents. Any errors or omissions are, of course, my own.

Chris Hellier
Ankara, 1993

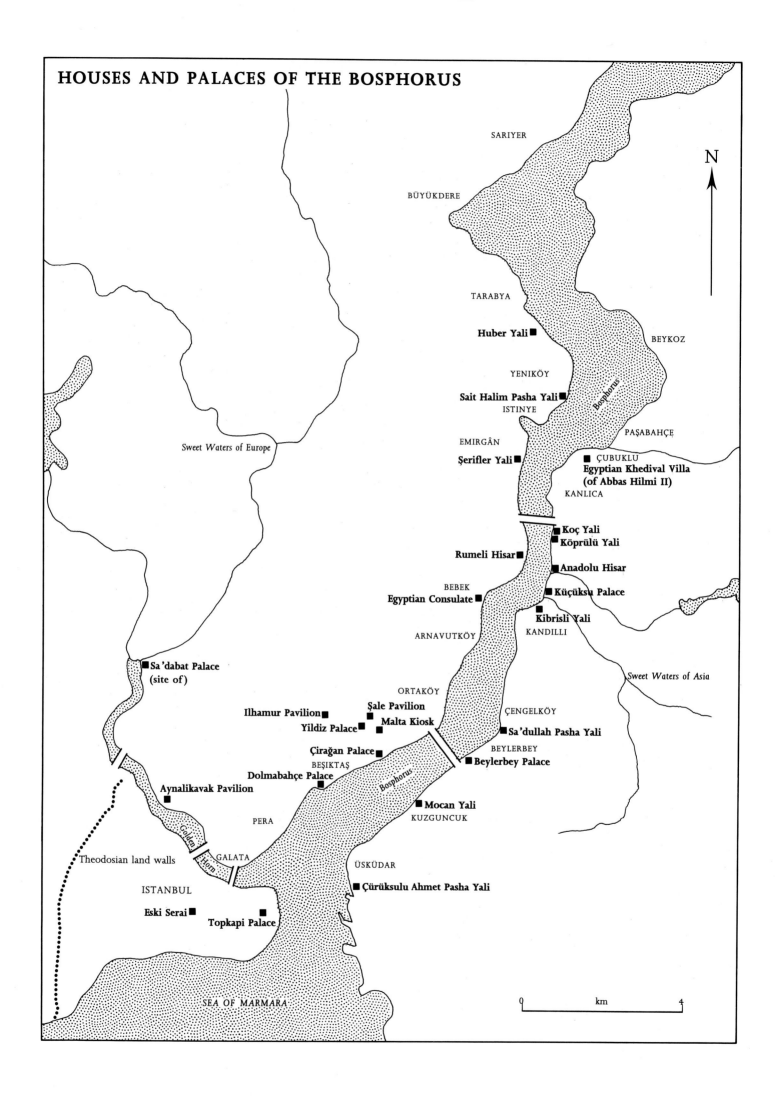

HOUSES AND PALACES OF THE BOSPHORUS

SARIYER

BÜYÜKDERE

N

TARABYA

BEYKOZ

Sweet Waters of Europe

YENIKÖY

Huber Yali ■

Bosphorus

Sait Halim Pasha Yali ■

ISTINYE

PAŞABAHÇE

EMIRGÂN

Şerifler Yali ■

■ ÇUBUKLU
Egyptian Khedival Villa
(of Abbas Hilmi II)

KANLICA

■ **Koç Yali**
■ **Köprülü Yali**

Rumeli Hisar ■

■ **Anadolu Hisar**

■ **Küçüksu Palace**

BEBEK

Egyptian Consulate ■

■ **Kibrisli Yali**

ARNAVUTKÖY

KANDILLI

■ **Sa'dabat Palace**
(site of)

Sweet Waters of Asia

ORTAKÖY

ÇENGELKÖY

Şale Pavilion

Ilhamur Pavilion ■

■

Yildiz Palace ■ ■ **Malta Kiosk**

■ **Sa'dullah Pasha Yali**

BEYLERBEY

Çirağan Palace ■

BEŞIKTAŞ

■ **Beylerbey Palace**

Dolmabahçe Palace ■

Bosphorus

Aynalikavak Pavilion ■

■ **Mocan Yali**

PERA

KUZGUNCUK

Golden Horn

Theodosian land walls

GALATA

ÜSKÜDAR

ISTANBUL

■ **Çürüksulu Ahmet Pasha Yali**

Eski Serai ■

■

Topkapi Palace

SEA OF MARMARA

0   km   4

CONTENTS

❖

1
ON THE WATERFRONT
page 9

2
THE GRAND SERAGLIO
page 31

Janissary Discontent 35 – Muhammad's Mantle 40
Forbidden Sanctuary 46 – Pools and Pavilions 50 – Legacy of the East 51
The Mark of Sinan 54 – Memorials to Victory 57 – Rococo and Tulips 61

3
WOODEN MANSIONS
page 79

Asian Origins 84 – Music By Moonlight 90 – Harems and Hamams 95
Tulips and Treaties 102 – A Theatre of the Baroque 111
Louis XVI and an Egyptian Prince 117 – Art Nouveau on the Bosphorus 129
Spirit of Impermanence 141

4
BEAUX-ARTS ON THE BOSPHORUS
page 151

The Balians and the New Architecture 154 – Fairy-Tale Flamboyance 182
A Touch of Arabia 185 – Dolphins in the Pool Room 194 – Road to Ruin 198

5
PAVILIONS IN A PARK
page 201

Chalet Chic 206 – A Picture Tells a Thousand Words 209
God's Shadow on Earth 210 – Exile and Revolt 214 – Palaces of the People 218

OTTOMAN SULTANS   222
GLOSSARY   223
BIBLIOGRAPHY   224
INDEX   226

1

--- ❖ ---

ON THE WATERFRONT

I am listening to Istanbul, intent, my eyes closed:
Still giddy from the revelries of the past,
A seaside mansion with dingy boathouses is fast asleep.

Orhan Veli Kanik, c.1940

The Bosphorus straits have captivated generations of travellers. Writers and poets as varied as Lady Mary Wortley Montagu and Lord Byron, Lamartine and Pierre Loti, have eulogized its forested shores sprinkled with palaces and ancient timber mansions. Even today, after decades of rampant urbanization, its remaining imperial residences, summer embassies, and pashas' homes paint a convincing picture of the city's glorious imperial past. The shores of the Bosphorus, its waters alive with ferries and fishing boats, motor launches and luxury yachts, are still one of the most enchanting aspects of this seductive three-in-one city: Byzantium-Constantinople-Istanbul.

Early accounts of the Bosphorus make curious and contradictory reading. According to classical tradition, Jupiter became enamoured with Io, the beautiful priestess of Juno, Jupiter's wife. Juno soon discovered her husband's deceit and in order to protect Io from the vengeful goddess he disguised his mistress as a beautiful heifer. Again Juno uncovered the fraud and ordered one of the Furies, a malicious gadfly, to pursue and torment her. Io wandered the earth in an attempt to flee the irritable pest and on her travels, still in the form of a cow, she crossed the straits separating Europe and Asia, giving the waters the name by which they have been known ever since – the Bosphorus, or 'Ford of the Cow'.

To Jason and the Argonauts the Bosphorus was no placid ford but a menacing stretch of water, the most dangerous section on their 2500-kilometre journey in search of the Golden Fleece. Rowing up the 29-kilometre straits against strong currents, fed by the waters of the Black Sea, the Danube, the Don, and other east European rivers, must have been a daunting task. The Argonauts struggled slowly on, weaving between current and counter-current, crossing from the European to the Asian shore in search of the least difficult passage.

Before Jason and his companions finally entered the dark expanse of the Black Sea they had to pass the menacing hurdle of the Cyanean or Clashing Rocks. Previous ships had been crushed in their stony jaws and if it had not been for the blind prophet Phineas, the *Argo* would have suffered the same fate. Phineas lived on the European bank of the Bosphorus, near the entrance to the Black Sea, where, with his ability to see into the future, he offered to help travellers. In order to negotiate the dreaded rocks successfully he instructed Jason to release a dove from

Iznik tile detail from the apartments of the sultan's mother, Topkapi Palace.

9

Argo. When she succeeded in flying between the rocks it was safe to follow and Jason and his crew continued on their next stage in search of the Golden Fleece.

Until recently historians doubted whether a late Bronze Age ship, powered only by human strength, could have successfully negotiated the strong currents of the Bosphorus. But in the mid-1980s the explorer Tim Severin, who has investigated the links between early voyages and mythology, proved that it was possible. With a multinational crew of oarsmen his latter-day *Argo* succeeded in edging its way up the straits, riding the counter-currents northwards.

The Bosphorus has spawned a number of lesser-known tales. Evliya Çelebi, the seventeenth-century Turkish traveller, believed the Bosphorus to be a canal 'which was cut by Alexander the Great to unite the Black and White Seas. The traces of this work,' he wrote, 'are even now to be seen on the rocks.' Perhaps these are the same marks that Petrus Gyllius, who served as a mercenary under Sultan Süleyman the Magnificent, referred to at Arnavutköy, on the European shore. Here he described 'stones worn down by a long procession of crabs' which, apparently unable to cope with the strong current, left the sea to cross a narrow promontory by land. The currents may have been too strong for Bosphorus crabs, but according to the classical lexicographer John Lemprière, human voices carried clearly across the wide straits. 'Cocks were heard to crow, and dogs to bark, from the opposite banks, and on a calm day persons could talk one to the other.'

The earliest communities to settle along the Bosphorus were groups of Megarians and Thracians, both Greek, who lived in the Chalcedon valley, present-day Kadiköy, from the seventh century BC. According to legend Byzas, the son of Poseidon and Keroessa, was inspired by the Delphic Oracle to found the New Acropolis at the southern entrance to the straits. Taking advantage of an opportunity missed by the Chalcedonians, Byzas encouraged another band of Megarians to seize the strategically important site of today's Topkapi Palace, Seraglio Point, where they soon established a new settlement as the hub of the fledgeling city.

More than a century later, in 512 BC, the first sizeable crossing of the Bosphorus occurred when Darius led a huge army against the Scythians. Darius ordered the construction of a bridge, designed by a Samian called Mandrocles. But before crossing the straits Darius sailed up the Bosphorus to the Clashing Rocks where he visited a temple of Hera overlooking the Black Sea. On his return he erected two marble columns, one inscribed in Assyrian, the other in Greek, naming the nations that took part in his campaign. Mandrocles was also commemorated. A picture showing Darius on his throne, the construction of the bridge, and the army crossing the strait, presented as an offering to the Hera temple, included the words: 'Goddess, accept this gift from Mandrocles, who bridged the Bosphorus' fish-haunted seas.'

Since then the Bosphorus, as both bridge and barrier, has played a central role in the shifting fortunes of the city that became successively Byzantium, Constantinople, and Istanbul. The city that has endured no fewer than twenty-two sieges, of which only six resulted in capture. The most celebrated, led by Sultan Mehmet the Conqueror in 1453, brought eleven centuries of Byzantine rule to an end and established Constantinople as the new capital of the growing Ottoman empire. An earlier, unsuccessful siege between 1396 and 1397 coincided with the construction of the Anatolian castle, the Anadolu Hisar, on the Asian side of the Bosphorus, built to control access to the Black Sea.

Over fifty years later Mehmet built the Rumeli castle, directly opposite the earlier fortification, further strengthening Ottoman control of the straits and preventing sea-borne aid reaching the city from the north, in particular, from the

ABOVE The rooftops of the harem and selamlik, Topkapi Palace, looking across the mouth of the Golden Horn and along the European shore of the Bosphorus. The palace stands atop one of the city's seven hills, Seraglio Point, an unrivalled vantage point and strategic location at the southern entrance to the straits.

BELOW The sixth-century Haghia Sophia, the church of Divine Wisdom, was the centre of religious life during the Byzantine Empire. Today, with its four minarets added to the basilica after the Turkish conquest, it stands as a reminder of the city's multifarious past.

OVERLEAF Rebuilt by Sultan Abdul Mecit, the Kuleli Officers' Training College on the Asian shore of the Bosphorus has been home to generations of budding army officers. Today a busy road winds its way along the shore, but in the early 1920s, 'there was silence all day long for none came to Kuleli save the students or the officers stationed there.' (Irfan Orga, Portrait of a Turkish Family, London, 1950)

Pontus kingdom with its capital at Trebizond, now in north-east Turkey. Completed in just four months, the castle is considerably bigger than its sister across the water, and was originally called Boğaz-kesen, literally 'cutter of the strait' or 'cut-throat' castle.

In February 1453, six months after the completion of the Rumeli fortification, Mehmet ordered his viziers to attack Constantinople. Ottoman soldiers and cannons were brought from Edirne to lead an assault on the city walls; an armada of ships in the Marmara Sea opened up a second marine front; while Ottoman armies from Anatolia crossed the Bosphorus for their new station on the European shore. Despite an already weak army, as well as political and religious divisions within the city, Byzantium managed to hold out against superior forces for forty-five days. A massive chain was stretched across the mouth of the Golden Horn, preventing the Turkish fleet from attacking the city's northern flank. But on the night of 21–22 April the Turks managed to drag several ships overland to the upper reaches of the Golden Horn. A month later, on 28 May, the final assault began. The Ottoman fleet broke the Byzantine chain, supplementing the foot soldiers who, in a matter of hours, breached the land walls and entered the city. The fall of Constantinople, or its conquest as the Turks prefer it, was a watershed in the history of the city. It soon became the new capital of the Ottoman empire and successive sultans embarked on an ambitious building programme, redesigning the city to suit the mores of its conquerors.

Initially Mehmet concentrated on raising the economic fortunes of the city by encouraging new settlers, Muslims, Greeks, Armenians, and Slavs, from the rest of the Ottoman empire. These were supplemented by European Jews eager to escape the latest wave of oppression in the west. After centuries of neglect during the later period of Byzantine rule much-needed roads, bridges, houses, markets, and workshops were constructed. In 1455 work began on the Kapali Çarşi, the famous Covered Bazaar, which was to remain the labyrinthine commercial heart of Istanbul until the middle of the twentieth century. Here traders met to sell and exchange wares from the four corners of the empire and beyond. Whole streets were occupied, and many still are, by rug and carpet salesmen, by turban-makers and jewellers, shoemakers and swordsmiths, by dealers in brass and copper and silk.

A new palace, a symbol of the sultan's enhanced power and achievements, was urgently required. After the conquest Mehmet built the Eski Serai, or Old Seraglio, a stone's throw from the bazaar, on a site occupied today by Istanbul University. Work soon began on a new palace, the illustrious Grand Seraglio at Topkapi Point, and the older official residence was gradually abandoned and fell into disrepair. Nothing remains of the original palace, but Topkapi Serai, much altered and added to over the centuries, still stands proudly atop the city's 'first hill', looking out over the Bosphorus straits and the narrow inlet of the Golden Horn.

Nearly a century after the conquest, in spring 1544, the Golden Horn witnessed one of the greatest receptions in Ottoman history: the return of Hayreddin Barbarossa, Sultan Süleyman the Magnificent's grand admiral, to a hero's welcome. Having sailed across the Sea of Marmara in his oared galley, the 'King of the Sea' passed below the new palace on Topkapi Point, and turned in to the Golden Horn. Lights hung from the minarets of the recently erected mosques and a multitude of people gathered to witness his historic homecoming. In ten years as the sultan's admiral, Barbarossa had reorganized the city's dockyards and rebuilt the Turkish navy into the strongest fleet in the Mediterranean. His navy had outwitted those of Spain, Venice, and France and been a crucial factor in spreading Ottoman suzerainty along the shores of north Africa.

A small wooden mosque south of the Kuleli Military School.

Just two years after his return to Constantinople, Barbarossa died in his palace on the Bosphorus and was buried in an octagonal tomb at Beşiktaş, a stone's throw from today's Dolmabahçe Palace. He remained a towering figure in Turkish history and in 1612 an Italian writer, Abbot Diego de Haedo, noted that he was 'held in such veneration among the Turks, particularly among the seafaring people, that no voyage is undertaken from Constantinople, by either public or private persons, without first visiting his tomb . . .' He is still a national hero, appearing frequently in schoolboy comics. Each day, commuters and office workers hurry past his tomb at Beşiktaş to catch the ferry bound for the Asian shore.

During Süleyman's reign only the most exalted Ottomans, such as Barbarossa, had their homes on the waterfront. Significant development of the Bosphorus shores did not occur until the beginning of the eighteenth century when, during a prosperous and light-hearted age known as the Tulip Period, after the fashion for cultivating the bulb, Sultan Ahmet III offered plots of land along the Bosphorus and Golden Horn to his relatives and members of the ruling élite.

Ahmet himself had a new pleasure palace, the Sa'dabat, or 'Place of Happiness', built on the upper reaches of the Golden Horn in a beautiful location known as the 'Sweet Waters of Europe'. Following Ahmet's extravagances, the upper classes and court ministers competed with each other in constructing palaces, gardens, fountains, and pavilions throughout Istanbul. The forested shores of the Bosphorus were the main beneficiary. Grand Vizier Daman Ibrahim Pasha, among the ablest of Ottoman ministers, having overseen the construction of Sa'dabat palace, had his own palace, a grand wooden yali, or waterfront mansion, built at Kandilli, a small village on the Anatolian shore. Others followed suit, raising wooden houses in the Turkish tradition, divided into a large selamlik, the men's quarters, and an adjoining harem for the women.

During Byzantine rule the city shoreline had been afforded special protection. According to a sixth-century ordinance:

> In this our royal city one of the most pleasant amenities is the view of the sea; and to preserve it we enacted that no building should be erected within a hundred feet of the sea front. This law has been circumvented by certain individuals. They first put up buildings conforming with this law; then put up in front of them awnings which cut off the sea view without breaking the law; next put up a building inside the awning; and finally remove the awning. Anyone who offends in this way must be made to demolish the building he has put up and further pay a fine of ten pounds of gold.

Under the Ottomans royal planners continued to guard the shoreline for the benefit of the sultan. At the end of the seventeenth century vacant building plots could still be found in old 'Stamboul and there was little pressure for development outside the Byzantine walls. But when Sultan Ahmet III finally allowed a selected élite to build along the Bosphorus no Byzantine-style restrictions were introduced preventing buildings abutting the sea. On the contrary, the ideal included sitting-rooms, lined with sofas, which projected over the straits, benefiting from their own sea views.

Ever since the first pasha established his home on the Bosphorus, a room with a view of the straits has commanded a substantial premium. Such is the desire for a Bosphorus home that it has generated a common Istanbul hypocrisy: improving your view at the expense of your neighbours and the public. The Byzantine edict quoted above would strike a pained note in the heart of a frustrated Istanbul planner today. Despite efforts to protect parts of the shoreline, illegal developments still squeeze their way between enraged neighbours, circumventing the political and bureaucratic obstacles. Early attempts to preserve important timber yalis were also thwarted by fire. Whether started by accident or arson, once alight, a brittle wooden yali could be razed to the ground in a matter of hours.

As the popularity of the Bosphorus grew Ottomans loved nothing better than to wander among its parks and gardens, picnicking by its shores whenever the weather permitted. In the imperial gardens gravel paths were lined with trees, with rows of fruit trees, borders of flowers, jasmine, and other shrubs. Their greatest delight was flowers. Ottoman poets praised the humble rose, believed to have been nurtured on the Prophet's sweat, and roses were keenly cultivated, as they still are in the southern city of Isparta, and made into jam, syrup, and rose-water. Even greater importance attached to the tulip which first appeared in Seljuk tiles in the twelfth century and subsequently had a prominent role in Ottoman decoration.

At the peak of Ottoman power at least 400 gardeners, according to one esti-mate, tended Topkapi's green acres, headed by the highly respected Bostancibaşi who had his own kiosk, or small pavilion, on the Marmara shore. Water played an important role in garden design. Fountains and pools were laid out next to the humblest kiosk and mature trees afforded shade behind high garden walls. During royal processions in the seventeenth century, elaborate floats, carried by slaves, included artificial gardens up to three metres square. Trees, flowers, and fruit were carefully modelled in wax; and clockwork engines pumped water through mini-ature fountains.

In the gardens of the seaside mansions the prolific writer Julia Pardoe, on a visit to Istanbul with her officer father in 1835, found rose trees

> . . . trained into a thousand shapes of beauty – sometimes a line of arches risen all bloom and freshness above a favourite walk – sometimes the plants are stretched round vases of red clay of the most classical formation, of which they preserve the shape – ranges of carnations, clumps of acacias, and bosquets of seringa, are com-mon; and the effect of these fair flowers, half shielded from observation, and overhung with forest trees, which are in profusion in every garden, is extremely agreeable.

Not all visitors, however, were attracted by Ottoman gardens. Even after nine years in Istanbul, a Frenchman, A. Brayer, writing about the same time as Julia Pardoe, could summon up little enthusiasm: 'Turkish gardens have nothing very unusual about them,' he wrote. 'The extraordinary features attributed to them are the products of the imagination of Europeans who love to envelop them in a mysterious oriental atmosphere.' Perhaps Brayer was looking with the wrong eyes. Turks preferred a natural informality, offset with parterres of coloured blooms and strategically placed pools, rather than the grand formalism of French gardens with which he, presumably, was more familiar.

The golden age of the 'true' Ottoman yali was the eighteenth century when a pure Turkish mansion, with roots in the distant past, developed on the forested shoreline. During the nineteenth century, however, Ottoman architectural conven-tions were increasingly abandoned or adapted to ideas imported from Europe, so that the Bosphorus developed a more cosmopolitan profile. Its inhabitants, too, were of mixed descent. In addition to wealthy Greeks, Armenians, and Jews, who built their own quarters in villages along the straits, the Bosphorus became a favourite summer retreat for the Egyptian aristocracy. Even after Turkey relin-quished control of Egypt to the British, upper-class Egyptians retained close

OPPOSITE Originally built by Sultan Beyazit I in 1391, the Anadolu Hisar ('Asian Fortress') was later strengthened by Mehmet the Conqueror in preparation for the 1453 siege of Istanbul.

LEFT The veteran cruiser Sarayburnu ('Seraglio Point'), moored in front of the Çirağan Palace Hotel.

BELOW At the narrowest point of the Bosphorus, Mehmet the Conqueror built the large Rumeli Hisar ('European Fortress') just four months before Constantinople fell to Turkish forces. With its sister fortress on the Asian shore, it controlled all traffic sailing along the straits.

relations with the Ottoman capital, educating their children in the city, marrying Ottoman ladies, and maintaining their spacious yalis.

Early Ottoman palaces were almost wholly built of wood and all, except the stone and timber Topkapi Serai, have disappeared. The earlier structures at Topkapi are among the few secular, imperial buildings to represent the period of 'classical' Ottoman architecture. Early Ottoman design was influenced by Byzantine, Persian, and Armenian traditions fused with native elements. There are no classical orders as in Graeco-Roman architecture, but two types of capital were typical: the lozenge and stalactite, a honeycomb-like formation derived from Seljuk architecture. At its best classical Ottoman architecture is an architecture of pattern and colour. Arches were pointed in Gothic fashion and interiors embellished in tiled panels of floral and vegetal designs. In the ceramic workshops of Iznik tile production reached its artistic peak between about 1570 and 1620, with secondary centres at Kütahya and Istanbul. After the mid-seventeenth century, however, the quality declined and Turkish ceramics were later replaced by inferior imports from Europe or by European imitations.

The rise and fall of Ottoman architecture was closely linked to the ruling dynasty. As the power of the Ottoman empire began to wane during the seventeenth and eighteenth centuries, the populace lost faith in the abilities of sucessive sultans and architecture began to look elsewhere for future direction. The classicism of Mimar Sinan, a near contemporary of Michelangelo, gave way to an indigenous baroque, an oratorical style derived, in part, through contacts with Europe. Turkish baroque nevertheless developed a distinct identity of its own, fused with earlier Ottoman traditions, and it reached its peak towards the middle of the eighteenth century, a century after the major baroque buildings of Europe. In baroque-influenced interiors the bombasticism inherent in the style was frequently tamed by, or contrasted with, the lighter decorative quality of rococo embellishment.

As the style of Ottoman yalis changed through increasing contacts with Europe, the old imperial serais along the Bosphorus were torn down and replaced by new palaces based on European models. Ottoman architectural tradition, typified by the stone kiosks and tiled interiors at Topkapi, were largely forgotten as nineteenth-century architects reintroduced an architecture based on Graeco-Roman aesthetics. The city's 'new' style was largely introduced by an Armenian family of architects, the Balians, who, as imperial architects, had the right to wear a gold set square and compass on their fez as a sign of their professional standing.

For centuries after the conquest of 1453 western classicism had had little place in the resurgent city. Classically educated travellers, unimpressed by Ottoman design, frequently complained that the Turks ignored the classical orders. 'They are little skill'd in the arts of which these lands were once the font,' wrote Byron, showing little appreciation for the native genius of Mimar Sinan. Yet if Byron had returned to the city just fifty years later he would have found a distinctly different imperial architecture that incorporated his venerated orders. When the sultans moved from Topkapi Palace in the mid-nineteenth century they effectively abandoned Turkish architectural traditions. The fluted columns and Corinthinian capitals of Ephesus and Pergamum were reinterpreted in the façades of Dolmabahçe and Beylerbey palaces and their imposing portals. Under the Balians, Graeco-Roman forms returned to Constantinople.

Like many European monarchs, sultans Abdul Mecit and Abdul Aziz sought to equal the incomparable court of Louis XIV and his successors. In nineteenth-century Europe official taste favoured the styles of classical antiquity and the

Built in 1903, *Haydarpasa railway station on the Asian shore is the main terminal for trains heading east and the Turkish end of the infamous Baghdad railway.*

Renaissance. Empress Eugénie of France, for one, helped to revive eighteenth-century court architecture and rococo decoration. Abdul Mecit followed the trend, raising the Italianate bulk of Dolmabahçe Palace on the European shore in 1856. But in many ways the capital's greatest building project of the century was a hollow gesture of illusionistic grandeur. The Ottoman empire was in dire financial straits, a situation exacerbated by the costs of prestigious new palaces.

In the sultans' Euro-palaces there was little that was distinctly Ottoman although there were concessions to tradition. Palaces remained divided into the selamlik and the harem. There was invariably a marble hamam, or Turkish bath, a room or two decorated in mother-of-pearl, and the occasional 'oriental' pool. But imported styles or products were no longer adapted to Ottoman forms: they replaced them. Vast oil paintings took the place of Turkish miniatures; Sèvres vases ousted Iznik ware; wallpaper and trompe-l'oeil effects displaced tiled panels. Recessed divans, where sultans had reclined to enjoy a pipe of Turkish tobacco or to appreciate poetry, were no longer suited to vast reception rooms where successive sovereigns received increasing numbers of foreign guests.

If Europeanization meant the end of indigenous design, it was even more unfortunate that the sultans chose to ape European palaces at a time when western art was itself in a state of malaise. European artists, uncertain about their future direction, took shelter in the revival of earlier artistic styles; while the arts and crafts tradition struggled against the threats of mass production.

Sultans Abdul Mecid and Abdul Aziz at least knew what they wanted: solid, classical statements of imperial power. But the last great sultan, the mysterious Abdul Hamid II, retreated from the Bosphorus shores and built his own palace at Yildiz, an eclectic warren of villas and curious kiosks. Architecturally, Yildiz Serai, the 'Palace of the Stars', became an expression of a culture in crisis and the dying days of empire. Abdul Hamid was past making grand gestures like his predecessors but he could still rise to the occasion, flattering European heads of state when the need arose by inaugurating new buildings. The visit of Kaiser Wilhelm II, in particular, was commemorated with the opening of the Şale Pavilion based on, of all possible models, a Swiss chalet.

To the Ottomans, European palaces were a powerful exotic lure, as exotic and intriguing as the Ottoman or Mughal courts were to the west. And there were parallel architectural influences. In Britain, the Prince of Wales, the future George IV, had tired of classicism and wanted something new. The result was John Nash's seaside pavilion at Brighton, a dazzling fun palace of Mughal domes and minarets built in 1815. Orientalist buildings and interiors, such as the Turkish boudoir at the Parisian Hôtel de Beauharnais, also sprouted in Germany and France. Pierre Loti, the romantic French novelist, recreated his personal interpretation of the Orient in his Rochefort house, complete with a Turkish sitting-room, an Ottoman mosque, and an Arabian salon. But these were one-off buildings, commissioned by eccentric writers, nostalgic colonial administrators, and experimental kings. By contrast the sultans' acceptance of western style, or what they believed to be western style, was almost wholesale, sacrificing the traditions of Sinan for the neoclassical western interpretations of the family Balian.

As well as radical developments in palace design the Bosphorus witnessed other changes during the nineteenth century. Foreign missions began to move from the traditional inland site of Belgrade Forest to the upper European shore. Major European powers built a long line of embassies in extensive gardens on land acquired from or granted by the reigning sultan. Stylistically they reflected the architecture

The forested shores of the Bosphorus and the oldest extant yali, the selamlik of the Köprülü mansion near Anadolu Hisar.

OVERLEAF *The mid-sixteenth-century Süleymaniye Camii, the mosque complex of Sultan Süleyman the Magnificent, is the largest in Istanbul and a dominant landmark above the Golden Horn.*

of their respective countries and have no place in the history of Ottoman architecture; nevertheless, they added to the cosmopolitan feel of the Bosphorus shores. Several of the embassies, including the distinctly Victorian British embassy, were destroyed by fire at the beginning of the twentieth century, but others still stand, an anachronistic symbol of the dying days of empire before the Turkish capital was moved to Ankara.

Marine traffic also underwent a rapid period of development under the later sultans. Wealthy yali owners, as well as the sultan and his entourage, were traditionally rowed up and down the Bosphorus in wooden caiques, a slow if pleasurable form of transport. The largest private caiques, in which dignitaries sheltered from the sun and rain beneath a silk canopy, had long, curving prows, often carved and painted. Regulations prescribed the number of oarsmen appropriate to the owner's rank, so that watchmen could easily identify approaching boats. Largest of all was the sultan's caique; a wave-cutting 28 metres long, it was pulled by forty oarsmen dressed in white. On Fridays, if the sultan was attending prayers by water, a royal procession of six caiques accompanied the sovereign to the nearest quay. In the boat following the sultan's sat the royal turban-bearer, with one of his master's cloth crowns, decorated with jewels and delicate feathers, held high.

Ordinary citizens could only marvel at such a lifestyle. For most people smaller, more rudimentary caiques made of polished beechwood, were the main means of transport. Long and frail, they were licensed to carry passengers from shore to shore for a fixed fee, and were supervised by a ferry master, usually a hajji, whose green turban proclaimed that he had made the pilgrimage to Mecca. The hajji also ensured that Islamic traditions were upheld. On the smaller caiques, men and women could only travel together if they were from the same family, while on the larger vessels, men and women were strictly segregated.

It was not until the 1840s that steam-powered ships began to replace the human-powered caiques, providing a regular and more rapid service from Istanbul to quays along the Bosphorus and to the Marmara Islands. A first class subscription service was started for wealthy officials and businessmen who lived out of town. And Sultan Mahmut II, the reformer, bought a steamship for his personal use on the Bosphorus and the Sea of Marmara. At first foreign companies, including British and Russian, operated ships between Ottoman and European ports. They also ran competing services along the straits, although these were forbidden after 1851 with the foundation of the Ottoman steamship company, the Şirket-i Hayriye, which was granted a monopoly over Bosphorus ferry sevices. Foreign companies, however, continued to provide most of the services along the Turkish shore of the Black Sea and to the Marmara coast.

Sailing up and down the Bosphorus, spotting the sultan's palaces and timber mansions, was, and still is, an essential part of any traveller's itinerary. One aristocratic visitor, the Comtesse de Gasparin, found herself stranded at Yeniköy without a boat in the early 1860s. She decided to walk back to the city with her husband and was delighted by the adventure. It was only their lazy companion, Pescator, who complained, allegedly out of concern for the lady's safety. The countess walked 'cheerfully' in the evening twilight, the Asian shore lit with the warm colours of dusk.

The threesome passed the gardens of large yalis, crossed cemeteries and parks and village squares. At the entrances to large houses eunuchs and guards enjoyed the fresh evening air. The countess saw at least one old pasha, chatting with his gardener, as he proceeded towards the harem with a basket of fresh peaches. At Arnavutköy, the Albanian village, sailors offered to row the countess the rest of the

OPPOSITE *An eclectic range of architectural styles seen in houses on the waterfront of the Asian shore of the Bosphorus.*

way to Constantinople but she politely declined, entranced by her evening stroll. For her the villages were a source of wonder, with the local seamen busying themselves about their boats and the small cafés lit by 'Aladdin's lamps'.

As well as castles and mosques, imperial palaces and timber yalis, the Bosphorus shores have spawned other notable landmarks. Perched on the hill above Harem, a cluttered container port on the Asian shore, stands the huge Scutari barracks originally constructed on the orders of Sultan Selim III and the scene of Florence Nightingale's ministrations during the Crimean War of 1854-6. During the conflict Harem was the point of disembarkation for boats carrying the wounded from distant battlefields.

Just north of Harem is one of the city's most familiar sights, Kiz Kulesi, or Maiden's Tower, standing on a tiny rock a few hundred metres offshore. In Turkish its name is derived from a variation on the distressed damsel folk tale. A royal astrologer foretold that a sultan's beautiful daughter would be bitten by a poisonous asp. In an attempt to place her out of harm's way, the sultan built an island retreat where she was to live, seen only by her eunuchs and ladies-in-waiting. But a Persian prince in the sultan's household had fallen for the girl and each evening he rowed to the island to offer her flowers. One summer evening he brought a whole basket of roses and lilacs (some say grapes), where, hiding beneath the fresh bouquets was a deadly asp. Inevitably it bit her but, like all good fairy-tales, the story has a happy ending; the prince saved his sweetheart by sucking the poison from her veins. In English the building is usually known as Leander's Tower, from a confusion between the Bosphorus and the Hellespont, across which Leander swam for clandestine meetings with his lover, the beautiful priestess Hero.

More impressive than Leander's Tower is the Germanic bulk of Haydarpasa railway station nearby. Built in 1903, during the golden age of rail travel, it is the principal terminal for the Anatolian network and the Turkish end of the infamous Baghdad railway. Although two road bridges have been built across the Bosphorus in the last twenty years, there is still no rail link. Passengers arriving from Europe on the resuscitated Orient Express must still transfer to a ferry if they wish to make an Asian connection. Inconvenient it may be, but it is a memorable way to begin a journey to the east.

For Istanbulites the Bosphorus remains unsurpassed as a residential and recreational area but the straits are also one of the most strategically important waterways in the world. Ottoman control of the Bosphorus went undisputed for three centuries after the fall of Constantinople. Then, as Russia gained a foothold along the northern shores of the Black Sea in the eighteenth century, Russian merchant vessels were granted free and unimpeded navigation. At the 1856 Treaty of Paris, bringing to an end the Crimean War, Britain and France pressed for the opening of the straits to merchant ships of all countries, although warships were still banned.

Turkey temporarily lost control of the straits when Allied troops occupied Istanbul after the First World War. The Bosphorus was subsequently demilitarized and placed under the control of an International Straits Commission which guaranteed navigational freedom to all ships. This did not please the Turks and in 1936 the Montreux Convention handed responsibility for administering the straits back to the Turkish government. The convention has regulated the passage of maritime traffic ever since, controlling the numbers of warships in the waterway at any one time, restricting night passage, and requiring advance clearance for certain types of vessels.

The agreement recognizes Istanbul's importance as a strategic crossroads where vital land and sea routes meet. Since the beginning of the city's history it has been a meeting-point of diverse communities, a melting-pot of cultures. They may not always have mixed well, but they have created a rich and varied mosaic. The modern city is still struggling to establish its own identity and Turkey is jostling for its place in the European Community. Its moves towards Europe, however, started a long time ago. When Abdul Mecit inaugurated his Euro-palace at Dolmabahçe in 1856 it was as if he was saying: 'Look! We're part of Europe.' A decade later Beylerbey Palace on the Asian shore yelled back: 'And so are we, but we still have a touch of the Orient.'

The Topkapi Palace rooftops and, down on the shore of the Golden Horn, the Sepetciler Kiosk. Built by Sultan Ibrahim in 1643, it is the only surviving summer palace, in what formed part of the seraglio garden, to have survived.

2

---✤---

THE GRAND SERAGLIO

When you go to the Seraglio you have to
enter by a gate which is very richly gilded,
and is called the 'Gate of Perpetual Delight'.
Sometimes you will see over it, stuck upon
the point of a pole, the head of a Grand Vizir,
or of some other personage, who has been
decapitated early in the morning, at the
caprice of the Grand Signor.

Anon, 1542

Mehmet the Conqueror's sprawling palace at Topkapi Point is still entered by the Gate of Perpetual Delight, more usually known as the Imperial Gate, a gateway that leads into the mysterious world of Ottoman intrigue, the secrets of the sultan's harem, and the most extensive example of Ottoman civil architecture ever built. Within its spacious courtyards are delightful stone kiosks, arabesque interiors of patterned tile, and ornate rococo rooms. The palace contains the third largest porcelain collection in the world, begun in 1504, and the most venerated of all Islamic treasures, the sacred relics of the Prophet Muhammad. Like most palaces it was built for the pleasure and protection of successive sovereigns and, as those severed heads on the 'Gate of Perpetual Delight' once reminded Istanbul's citizens, as a symbol of despotic rule.

When Mehmet the Conqueror commissioned his new palace at Topkapi Point his architects followed the tradition of flexible courtyard design that had been established in earlier palaces, now demolished, at Bursa and Edirne. The palace walls created a framework within which Mehmet's successors could indulge their own whims and fancies, adding new buildings to suit the latest sultanic taste. As it stands today, the palace was built over several artistic periods, encompassing classical Ottoman design, the freshness of the Tulip Period, and the exuberance of the baroque. During the 400 years that it was the centre of the sultanate new apartments and kiosks were gradually added. Among the first, the fifteenth-century Tiled Kiosk reflected the Turks' central Asian origins; the last addition, the Europeanized kiosk of Sultan Abdul Mecit erected in 1840, displayed increasing western influence.

From the outside Topkapi Serai, literally the 'Cannon Gate Palace', lacks the grandeur associated with European palaces. It is an inward-looking complex, concerned essentially with its own private world, shut off from its subjects by imposing gateways and mammoth stone walls. Except for the harem and the fourth court, its plan remains largely as it was during the reign of Fatih Mehmet.

The rooftops of the labyrinthine harem and selamlik quarters of Topkapi Palace. Across the Golden Horn inlet lie the districts of Pera and Galata, once known as the European quarter of the city.

31

Once known as the Gate of Salutation, the medieval-looking central gate leads
into the inner courts of Topkapi Palace. Only the sultan was allowed to ride
through the gate; others, including visiting ambassadors and senior functionaries,
had to dismount and, with due humility, enter the Divan Court on foot.

The Divan Tower rises above a room where meetings of the public divan, the state council, were held four times a week. Although damaged by fire and rebuilt on several occasions the tower's form and location remain as they were in the late fifteenth century.

Built during the nineteenth century, the *Alay Kiosk* stands on the site of earlier pavilions where successive sultans gathered to watch the passing of the guilds. On Fridays the sultan and his entourage met here before leaving for noon-time prayers at the mosque. It was also the scene of more bloody events. During a Janissary revolt in 1655 Mehmet IV attempted to appease his rebellious troops by hurling the bodies of his Chief Black and White Eunuchs from the windows.

Mural paintings depicting small country kiosks decorate the façade of the Gate of Felicity, also known as the 'Gate of the White Eunuchs'.

Serious fires ravaged sections of the palace on at least three occasions, in 1574, 1665, and again in 1856. Many of the earliest buildings have thus disappeared, including most of those in the first court, or were reconstructed to such an extent that they belong to a later artistic period.

Based on a distinct spatial and social hierarchy, the relatively public first court leads, via processional paths, to the privacy and intimacy of the third and fourth courts beyond. The courts also correspond to the functions carried out by the extensive palace staff. The first court, sometimes known as the Courtyard of the Janissaries, was a service area for the palace, including a hospital for the pages of the Palace School; an imperial bakery, now workshops associated with the museum; an arsenal; the Imperial Mint and the Outer Treasury. Subsidiary buildings were used as storage areas or dormitories for members of the outer service, such as domestics and guards, of whom at least fifty were on duty at any one time. There were also areas for the Carriers of Silver Pitchers, the Straw Weavers, and others whose humble tasks precluded them from contact with inner, residential areas.

JANISSARY DISCONTENT

The first court was open to all, yet, despite the crowds that gathered here, many visitors remarked un the uncanny silence maintained by the palace guards. The French traveller Joseph Pitton de Tournefort, writing in the early eighteenth century, noted that 'the Motion of a Fly might be heard' and 'the very Horses seem to know where they are, and no doubt they are taught to tread softer than in the streets.'

The rule of silence, however, was frequently broken by the increasingly rebellious Janissary corps in defiant displays of military power. This élite, the first professional army in Turkish history, was probably founded towards the end of Mehmet the Conqueror's reign, although groups of captured Christians had served earlier sultans as bodyguards. In the vicinity of the sultan's palace or on the battlefield their dark blue coats were instantly recognizable. Striking boots coloured red, yellow, or black indicated the wearer's rank. Most curious of all were their tall felt hats which flapped down behind, reaching to the middle of the back. Older members of the corps crowned their hats with bird-of-paradise feathers. Beards were forbidden, but bushy moustaches enhanced their warlike image.

Janissary recruits came from all conquered states but particularly from Bosnia, Bulgaria, and Albania. The most promising were educated at the Palace School with the majority trained for combat through hard manual labour. Their role called for unquestioning obedience. Marriage was not permitted, and strict observance of their adopted religion was enforced. During peacetime they received no wages and were confined to barracks. Such rules, isolating them from normal social relations, reinforced their loyalty to the sultan and to their fellow soldiers.

During the earlier years of Janissary history they were an effective fighting force, crucial to the expansion of Ottoman borders. But before long dissatisfaction, prompted by inadequate rations and social constraints, led to the widespread breaking of rules. Janissaries began to marry and their children were accepted into the corps, increasing the proportion of unsatisfactory soldiers and weakening their loyalty to the sultan. From the seventeenth century their numbers, power, and independence grew considerably, leading to the Janissary deposition or murder of six sultans. Janissary revolts became an increasingly common feature of Ottoman history, their rebelliousness associated with acts of arson. During Ahmet III's twenty-seven-year reign in the early eighteenth century, 140 fires were attributed

A colonnade of different marbles runs in front of the Hall of the Pantry in the third court.

Pebbled floors, inherited from Byzantine tradition, frequently decorated porticoes and principal courtyards.

The Pavilion of the Holy Mantle houses some of the most venerated of Islamic treasures to be found anywhere. As well as Muhammad's cloak, seized by Sultan Selim I after the capture of Cairo in 1517, the Prophet's sacred standard, hairs from his beard, an alleged footprint, a tooth, and a personal seal are all displayed here.

ABOVE Detail of a cupboard inlaid with mother-of-pearl
and flanked by elaborate decorated tiles.

RIGHT Interior view of the apartments of the Sultane Valide.

to Janissary discontent alone. By the early nineteenth century their numbers had risen to 130,000, from just 20,000 three centuries earlier. They had become a law to themselves and were out of control.

In the irregular first court a large plane tree once stood where dissatisfied Janissaries gathered to protest against their conditions by overturning large copper kettles. Ringleaders were frequently rounded up and hanged from the tree's branches. Several sultans attempted to reorganize the force, but more radical measures were called for; and they were finally crushed in 1826 when Mahmut II masterminded a bloody slaughter in the hippodrome square.

From the Courtyard of the Janissaries, the imposing Middle Gate, or Gate of Salutations, leads into the second court and the mysteries of the Inner Palace. At this juncture anyone with business to transact with the palace was obliged to dismount: only the sultan was allowed to ride beyond this point. The second court was the preserve of the Divan, or Imperial Council, responsible for the administration of the empire and it was here that the council met four times a week to dispense its rough justice.

While surrounded by several peripheral complexes housing the Council Chamber, the Inner Treasury, the Public Relations Office, and the Office of the Grand Vizier, the second court was essentially a parade ground. Its principal paths were lined with slender cypress trees and on the spacious lawns gazelles roamed freely and peacocks preened their feathers. Almost as colourful as the peacocks were the displays of imperial pageantry when costumed officials, palace guards, and thousands of Janissaries assembled for public meetings of the council.

MUHAMMAD'S MANTLE

The aptly named Sultan's Way slices through the second court and leads to the third portal, the Gate of Felicity, and the strictly private areas of the palace beyond. The third court was reserved for court and government officials and includes the principal halls of the Palace School, a rigorous training ground for the imperial civil service. Youths schooled at this élite institution were conscripted from Christian minorities within the empire and their success as administrators was a major contribution to the efficient running of the Ottoman empire during its earlier golden age. Other important buildings in the third court include parts of the selamlik or sultan's reception rooms; the black eunuchs' quarters; the library of Ahmet III, dating from 1719; and the Hirkei Şerif Odasi, or 'Pavilion of the Holy Mantle', containing relics of the Prophet Muhammad.

This shrine contains the most revered objects in the palace and is visited by pious Muslims from all over the world. Most sacred of all is the Prophet's cloak which, according to tradition, Muhammad gave to an Arab poet, Ka'b ibn Zuhayr, whom he sought to convert to Islam. After the poet's death, his children sold the mantle to the founder of the Ummajid dynasty, Mu'awiweh I. It was subsequently transferred to Baghdad, then to Egypt, where the titular Caliphs held court in Cairo. But the warring Sultan Selim I had designs on the traditional centres of Islam and in 1516-17 his armies swept south through the Arab lands, through Syria and across the Sinai peninsula to the outskirts of Cairo. After several days of fierce fighting in which thousands lost their lives, Selim captured the partially destroyed city and with it the Prophet's relics. Selim adopted the title of Caliph, emphasizing the Ottoman role as leaders and defenders of the faith, and the Prophet's mantle and other relics were transferred to Topkapi Palace where the Hirkei Şerif Odasi was built specially for them.

The Courtyard of the Sultane Valide became the focus of the sultan's mother's apartments. The most powerful woman in the Ottoman Empire, the queen mother consolidated her position through deft intrigue, ruling the harem and the life of her son's women with a will of iron.

The alley or Courtyard of the Black Eunuchs runs through the black eunuchs' quarters, connecting the harem with the third court. The black eunuchs gradually usurped the power of their rivals, the white eunuchs, and their chief, the Kislar *Aga*, was the inspector of religious endowments as well as 'Chief of the Girls'.

The Black Eunuchs' Courtyard looking south.

During the rest of Ottoman history the relics were closely guarded and displayed only on important state occasions. On the fifteenth day of Ramadan, the holy mantle was shown to the court and, one by one, the assembled crowd kissed it. The Kislar Aga, the Chief Black Eunuch, then washed the mantle in a silver bowl, poured the resultant holy water into small phials and distributed it to the fasting faithful. At the end of the fast a few drops of holy water added to a glass of water in the evening was believed to protect against illness and ensure divine salvation. The mantle was left to dry until the twentieth day of Ramadan and then returned to its coffer, where it lies today beneath a golden baldachin.

Second only in importance to the holy mantle is the sacred standard, which did not reach Constantinople until 1595. According to popular tradition the standard had been a turban-winder belonging to one of the Prophet's converted enemies; others believe it served as a curtain covering the tent door of Muhammad's favourite wife, Ayesha. Whatever its true origins, after his conquest of Egypt, Selim I sent the standard to Damascus where it was carried each year at the head of a procession of pilgrims on their way to Mecca. Soon it came to symbolize Ottoman power and was unfurled during times of war; the last occasion during which Turkey proclaimed a holy war was against the Allies in 1915.

The revered pavilion also contains hairs from the Prophet's beard, reputedly shaved after his death by his favourite barber, Salman. Other hairs are venerated in India and Tunisia, where three whiskers are preserved in the so-called Mosque of the Barber near Kairouan. There is also one of Muhammad's teeth, one of the four he lost after being struck by an axe at the Battle of Bedr, a footprint, and personal seal. To these were added swords belonging to the first four Caliphs, ancient Korans, and a door from the great mosque at Mecca.

At the entrance to the third court stands the Throne Room, the essential symbol of sovereign power, where decisions taken by the Divan received the royal assent. After meetings of the Imperial Council, the Grand Vizier or other senior functionaries passed through the Gate of Felicity and reported to the sultan in his tent-shaped room with its roof projecting over a wrap-around portico and supported on twenty-four columns. The Throne Room dates back to the reign of Mehmet the Conqueror but was remodelled by several later sultans, most recently after a devastating fire in 1856. The only elements to have survived from the sixteenth century are a fine marble fountain near the principal entrance, inlaid with swirls of porphyry; the gilt-bronze chimney; and the throne's magnificent canopy. Broad moulding along the baldachin, decorated with lacquered work in the 'saz' style, an ornamentation of Asian origin, is composed of gilded motifs painted green and black on a dark red background. Dragons and the mythical simurg bird, ancient symbols of immortality, fight amidst stylized vegetation.

Visiting ambassadors presented their credentials and gifts to the sultan at the Gate of Offerings, the entrance fronting the Gate of Felicity. Lord Byron and his close associate John Cam Hobhouse presented themselves here when accompanying the British ambassador to an audience with Sultan Mahmut II in the early nineteenth century. Hobhouse was overawed by 'that indescribable majesty which it would be difficult for any but an Oriental sovereign to assume'.

His attendant white eunuch took him to within ten paces of the throne where he held him tightly by the right arm throughout the proceedings. Mahmut sat motionless on his dazzling throne, rolling his eyes from side to side. He was dressed in a robe of yellow satin, bordered with sable, and carried a diamond-covered dagger. On his head he wore a white and blue turban plumed with bird-of-paradise feathers. After a brief audience of ten or fifteen minutes the sultan

Tile and door details in the Black Eunuchs' Courtyard.

Tiles decorated with cypress trees in the Black Eunuchs' Courtyard.

Tile panels in the notorious 'Cage' or 'Prison of the Princes' where generations of princes were confined to prevent their challenging the ruling sultan for the throne.

45

retired. Hobhouse's eunuch hurried him out of the room, and dismissed him 'with a gentle push down the steps of the ante-chamber'.

FORBIDDEN SANCTUARY

To the west of the third and fourth courts lies the maze of the harem, the most notorious of palace institutions. The quarters of the imperial household comprise some 300 rooms leading off passageways, courtyards, gardens, and staircases. Early descriptions of the harem were often imaginary or based on hearsay, making it difficult to assess its exact size, but one seventeenth-century writer estimated that there were 2000 men and women in the household, of which up to 1200 were concubines. The women were served by hundreds of black eunuchs, seized from the upper reaches of the Nile and swiftly castrated before being assigned to the palace under the control of the Master of the Virgins.

At times the sultan's ladies must have suffered from extreme boredom idling away their days confined to the harem, playing music, singing, dancing, and sewing. They were mostly foreign girls, taken from their homelands during Ottoman conquests. On entering the harem they were obliged to convert to Islam with the simple pronouncement that 'There is no God but God alone, and Muhammad is his prophet.'

A hierarchy soon developed among the harem women with some favourites wielding considerable power. Those who particularly pleased the sultan were showered with presents of money and jewels, commensurate with the degree of satisfaction they gave. A girl who caught the eye of the sultan became a *gözde*. If she was called to share the imperial bed a second time she reached the status of an *ikbal*, who, if she gave birth, became a *haseki* and received her own special apartments and servants.

This closeted existence, built essentially on lust, was a breeding ground for jealousy, fear, and murder. Punishment for insolence could be severe and any woman suspected of witchcraft was tied in a sack and cast, screaming, out to sea. One particularly cruel sultan, Ibrahim 'the mad', simply tired of the same young faces and, to make room for a fresh stock of available nymphs, drowned his entire harem off Seraglio Point.

Adopted from an Arabic word meaning 'unlawful', the harem came to imply a woman's sanctuary or territory 'forbidden' to men, except, of course, for the master of the house. The harem was governed by a complex set of rules with the sultan's mother, the Sultane Valide, having supreme power, taking control of her son's wives and concubines and organizing their daily lives. Other women could also rise to positions of influence. After the death of Süleyman the Magnificent's mother, a Russian slave captured by Crimean Tartars, Roxelana, known as Haseki Hurrem in Turkey, exerted a powerful hold over the longest reigning sultan in Ottoman history. After becoming his legal wife Roxelana consolidated her power by transferring the harem from the Old Seraglio to Topkapi Palace. Here she continued to crave power and sought the right of succession for one of her four sons. She became known as the 'witch' and, after a series of dastardly deeds, finally persuaded Süleyman to execute his eldest son, Mustafa, on the grounds that he had been plotting against his father. By killing his successor Süleyman opened the door for Selim II, 'the Sot', Roxelana's own son, to succeed him on the throne.

Other potential heirs to the throne often met their maker in the shadows of the harem. It was common practice, indeed a right stipulated by Mehmet II, for ascending sultans to murder their brothers to prevent any challenge to the throne.

Upper windows, such as this one in the 'Cage', were frequently glazed in coloured glass casting pools of coloured light on the marble floors.

RIGHT *From their locked apartments, known appropriately as the 'Cage' or 'Princes' Prison', successive Ottoman princes looked out over the Courtyard of the Cage. Unaware of the affairs of state or the realities of the outside world, they were detained for years on end to prevent any challenge to the Ottoman throne.*

OPPOSITE ABOVE Architecturally the most important part of the seraglio, the fourth court includes a tranquil fountain and pool, one of the palace's original features which was remodelled during the seventeenth century. To the left, beyond the covered walkway, stands the Revan Pavilion, built in 1636 following the Ottoman capture of Erivan.

OPPOSITE BELOW Mimar Sinan, the most accomplished of classical Ottoman architects, redesigned the palace kitchens after a serious fire in 1574. Replacing the roof with a row of ten double domes and tall chimneys he produced a dramatic silhouette of rhythmic elegance.

LEFT The Çinili Kiosk, the oldest free-standing structure in the serai, built in 1472, was influenced, notably in its inlaid decor, by Timurid architecture of central Asia. Its cruciform plan, with four corner rooms, formed a model for later buildings at Topkapi Point and for early yalis along the Bosphorus, and was reinterpreted in the plans of the nineteenth-century Euro-palaces.

Mehmet III had all nineteen of his brothers put to death, and drowned his father's pregnant concubines lest they produced another future threat to his reign.

The princes' apartments, known more appropriately as the Kafes, or 'Cage', were also located near the harem. Some future sultans spent most of their life confined to the 'Princes' Prison', their cloistered lives relieved, occasionally, by the sultan's barren concubines. This must have been inadequate recompense for Osman II who spent fifty years in the Kafes before ascending to the throne aged fifty-five and with only three more years to live. Other sultans, disgraced or incompetent rulers, were deposed and retired to quiet back-room apartments to live out their remaining days with the fear of death, at the hands of the new sultan or senior bureaucrats, hanging over their heads.

POOLS AND PAVILIONS

No imperial gateway marks the transition from the third to the fourth courts. Instead narrow alleyways lead to the last enclosure, an area of gardens, including the tulip garden of Ahmet III, and assorted kiosks laid out among a network of pathways and marble steps. Here stand the Baghdad and Revan kiosks built to commemorate Ottoman success in battle. Between them lies an ornate fountain rising from the centre of a shallow pool and, to the west, a marble terrace with a gilt-bronze canopy looking out up the Golden Horn and across this narrow inlet to Pera and Galata to the north. This must surely have been the most pleasant and quietest corner for the later sultans to relax, wandering among the beds of tulips, the soothing sprinkling of the fountains easing the pressures of ruling an extensive empire.

Long before the fourth court took its present form, the open 'L'-shaped hall, flanking the Pavilion of the Holy Mantle, was witness to one of the strangest meetings between east and west. In 1599, Thomas Dallam gave an organ recital here on a fine 'instrumente' presented to the sultan on behalf of Queen Elizabeth I of England. At the time Mehmet III had recently ascended the throne, English trading rights with the Sublime Porte were due for renewal, and Queen Elizabeth, toying with the idea of an alliance with the Turks to combat the strength of the Spanish navy, sought the sultan's attention with congratulatory letters and ostentatious presents. Chief among these was the organ, despatched and paid for by the Levant Company, sent from London, along with Dallam, to Constantinople. After arriving in the city Dallam spent days on end returning to the fourth court at Topkapi where he carefully reconstructed the royal gift.

In the account of his experiences, the first description of the Grand Seraglio by an outsider, Dallam described the pillared hallway where the organ began to take shape as a 'great house' flanked by two rows of marble pillars with pedestals of brass and gilt.

> The wales on three sides of the house ar waled but halfe waye to the eaves; the other halfe is open; but yf any storme or great wynde should hapen, they can sodonly Let fale suche hanginges made of cotten wolle for that purpose as will kepe out all kinds of wethere, and sudenly they can open them againe. The fourthe side of the house, which is close and joynethe unto another house, the wale is made of purfeare, or suche kinde of stone as when a man walketh by it he maye se him selfe tharin . . . Thare weare in this house nether stouls, tables, or formes, only one coutche of estate. Thare is one side of it a fishe ponde, that is full of fishe that be of divers collores.

On the day appointed for the official presentation the sultan arrived at Seraglio Point in the royal caique. Eager to see his present, he hurried up the hill to the palace where 400 of the palace staff making a 'wonderfull noyes' awaited him. Dallam had set the organ and, as Mehmet took the throne, 'the clockes strouke 22; than the chime of sixteen bels went of, and played a songe in 4 parts.' Palace musicians replied with the sound of two silver trumpets. Then the organ struck up a second time followed by 'a holly bushe full of blackbirds and thrushis . . . (which) did sing and shake their wynges' and 'divers other motions . . . which the grand Sinyor wondered at.' The sultan seemed pleased with his new gift but asked how the keys could move when nothing touched them. At this point Dallam was summoned to play and the sultan moved to one side so that he could watch the musician's hands. For Dallam's self-proclaimed 'good suckcess' he received forty-five pieces of gold and was invited to stay on in Turkey as the sultan's organist. But Dallam declined the offer and sailed back to England in November, the first occidental musician to be received in the sultan's court.

LEGACY OF THE EAST

Apart from the fifteenth-century walls and the imperial gateways, typical of the military architecture of the time, few of the original palace buildings still stand. The only one of major importance, a rare survivor and the oldest secular building in the city, is the Tiled Pavilion, or Çinili Kiosk, an outer pavilion lying in the grounds of the serai. Built in 1472, it is an elegant building originally raised up on narrow wooden columns which were replaced by stone pillars in the eighteenth century. It has none of the massiveness associated with some of Mehmet II's other buildings, such as the Janissary barracks or the first Eyup mosque, now dismantled, or the grand scale of the palace walls, indicative of the soldier and 'the conqueror'. Its sumptuous decor of patterned tiling in deep blue and turquoise, and its apparent lightness, reflects, perhaps, another side of the sultan, the private side of a ruler needing a retreat near at hand.

The kiosk also appears to have been built for entertainment, with a viewing platform and recessed entrance looking out over what was a large jirit field. Jirit was popular with sultans as well as their subjects. It was a risky sport, a form of javelin throwing played on horseback, a cross between polo and a medieval joust, in which opposing teams attempted to hit each other with blunted sticks.

Architecturally the Tiled Pavilion is a crucial building in the evolution of Ottoman design. Derived from Timurid models, the axial plan has a cruciform central salon, with a smaller room in each of the four corners. The plan was frequently repeated in later buildings, in town houses and in the grand seventeenth- and eighteenth-century yalis along the Bosphorus. It was also adapted for use in the nineteenth-century Euro-palaces at Dolmabahçe and Beylerbey. Stylistically, particularly in the inlaid decor, the kiosk borrows from Timurid architecture of central Asia and has been attributed to an unknown Iranian architect. On three sides of the vault a long Persian inscription, written in the 'cuerda seca' technique, gives the date of construction. Tiles in cuerda seca, literally 'dry cord', were decorated with coloured glazes which were prevented from running together by a thin line of potash permanganate. Rooms lead off the central domed area where fireplaces are built into the white plaster walls. Today it is impossible to say if earlier Ottoman palaces included similarly styled kiosks, but the Tiled Pavilion suggests a break with the past and the beginning of a new era heralded by the conquest of Istanbul.

ABOVE In Murad III's bedroom a three-tiered fountain played a liquid tune to accompany the sultan's amorous pleasures.

RIGHT The bedroom of Murad III, where the sultan enjoyed the favours of a Venetian beauty called Safieh. She later wielded great influence in the running of the Ottoman empire and conspired in the murder of Mehmet III's nineteen brothers. Her plotting, however, made her many enemies within the seraglio and she was finally strangled while asleep.

While Mehmet the Conqueror provided the framework within which the imperial palace could expand it was left to other sultans to fill in the pieces of the complex architectural jigsaw puzzle that became the Grand Seraglio. The task of moving the Ottoman government from Edirne to Istanbul was only completed during the reign of Selim I, 'the Grim' (1512–20), who transferred soldiers and scribes to Topkapi Palace. Already, however, the palace was becoming rather cramped. In order to expand the Janissary corps Selim built a new school, with barracks, medrese, mosque, and kitchens, at Galatasaray, thus vacating their previously inadequate quarters at the palace. Selim also built a small palace, the Yali Kiosk, on the shores of the Marmara, a place of solitude for the sultan and his chosen women. Like Mehmet, Selim was a great conqueror and his short reign an undoubted success in military terms. But the peak of Ottoman grandeur had not yet been reached.

THE MARK OF SINAN

The title of 'the Sultan of Sultans, king of kings . . . God's shadow on earth, emperor and sovereign lord of the White Sea and the Black Sea . . .' belongs to Selim's successor, the larger-than-life figure of Sultan Süleyman the First, whose reign represented the peak of artistic endeavour as well as Ottoman power. To the west he was the true 'Grand Turk', 'the Magnificent', although the Turks prefer to remember him as 'the Lawgiver'. His reign is associated with luxury and ostentatious splendour, but he was also a wise and energetic sultan comparable in stature to his European contemporaries such as François I of France and Emperor Charles V. His fondness for jewels became legendary when he rode on to the battlefield wearing a turban studded with diamonds. He commissioned a gold throne bedecked with topaz, emerald-hafted daggers, and an extraordinary Venetian helmet – especially designed to catch the eye of visiting dignitaries – inset with diamonds, pearls, rubies, emerald, and turquoise. Miniature painting thrived under Süleyman's patronage, while Iznik ceramics approached their most illustrious phase. Yet, among all the artistic achievements of Süleyman's reign, the golden age of Ottoman art belongs to architecture and to the work of Mimar Sinan, one of the world's greatest architects.

Sinan, a near contemporary of Palladio, was appointed Royal Chief Architect by Süleyman when in his late forties, after serving as the general of the engineers where he designed and restored bridges for the army. His best work represents the zenith of classical Ottoman architecture, comparable to the High Renaissance in Europe. He produced a remarkable variety of mosque designs, invariably memorials to great statesmen or members of the royal family, creating perfect unified spaces beneath towering domes and slender minarets. Among his greatest contributions to Ottoman art were his elaborate interiors where, displaying a new confidence in the use of materials, walls and niches were richly decorated in a stunning variety of patterned tiles. Sinan's best and most celebrated work were his monumental mosque designs, such as the Süleymaniye complex completed in 1557, and still a dominant feature towering above the Golden Horn.

As Chief Royal Architect Sinan was responsible for additions and extensions to Topkapi Palace. His monumental statements were clearly unsuitable for the smaller-scale, intimate character of the serai, although a number of notable additions display his unquestionable genius. When the palace kitchens were badly damaged by fire in 1574 Sinan rose to the challenge of reconstructing such prosaic buildings with a restrained monumentality. Their plan remained largely

Tile panels in the apartments of the sultan's mother include depictions of the Ka'aba, the building at Mecca containing the sacred black stone.

unchanged but in order to overcome the problem of poorly ventilated kitchens, he replaced the roof with a row of ten double domes capped by tall chimneys. The result, 'the most sublime part of the seraglio' according to William Makepeace Thackeray, is an eye-catching silhouette, a practical response of rhythmic elegance, best appreciated as one approaches Istanbul from the Marmara Sea.

The first major buildings of the Topkapi harem were built towards the end of Sinan's long career. Little remains as originally designed by the prolific master except for the classical Ottoman bedroom of Murad III, hidden away like a lost jewel among the gloom of the ladies' labyrinth. For Murad, the grandson of Süleyman and the last sultan for whom Sinan worked, he produced one of the most outstanding of Ottoman interiors, described by Lesley Blanch in *Pavilions of the Heart* as 'the loveliest of all rooms for loving'. Appropriately, the privy chamber is dominated by a pair of huge canopied beds, each carved and gilded, flanking a tall hearth, typical of those found in old Turkish houses. A conical bronze hood, reminiscent of protective helmets worn by Asian warriors, or, to western eyes, a witch's hat, caps the fireplace, the *ocak*, where a warm glow kept the chill off the royal love-nest on winter evenings.

On the opposite wall stands a three-tiered marble fountain, symbolically essential for joy and relaxation, where nine bronze taps played their liquid tunes. Each tap sounded a different note, producing a veritable symphony to accompany imperial love-making. Circling the room a broad strip of Koranic inscriptions, 'The Verse of the Throne', unifies the four walls, each treated in scintillating panels of Iznik faience. The most striking tiles, set above the calligraphic dado, grow into flowering tulips, carnations, and vegetal patterns against a deep blue background, edged with the coral red characteristic of Iznik ware.

Stripped of its soft furnishings, its floor of bare stone, the room appears cold today, lacking the luxuriousness it must have revealed in Murad's time. Gone are the sumptuous velvet hangings, black and white and violet, embroidered with pearls and rubies, emeralds and turquoise. Gone, too, is the collection of carpets, brought from Konya, Denizli, or Karabagh, a colourful patchwork covering for Murad's slippered feet, an effect reinforced by the coloured light filtering down from the stained-glass windows. The baldachin beds, true royal four-posters, where Murad entertained his favourite concubine, Safieh Baffo, would also have been spread with cushions.

The splendour of the room was matched by the beauty of Safieh who, for years, was Murad's only concubine, a rare honour indeed among the promiscuous sultans. A stunning Italian of noble Venetian stock, she was abducted by corsairs and sold a love slave into the seraglio. There she soon drew the attention of the sultan's mother, the Sultane Valide, who selected her as a suitable virgin for her son on the evening of the *bayram*, the 'Night of Power'. Safieh may have become Murad's favourite but she was still expected to display humility in the ruler's presence, even in the privy chamber, entering the bed from the bottom and inching up slowly between the covers.

MEMORIALS TO VICTORY

Murad III's bedroom was Sinan's last significant contribution to the palatial compound at Topkapi. After his death in 1588 Ottoman architecture had passed its glorious peak. The following century, a period of fluctuating fortunes and increasing political uncertainty, nevertheless produced some remarkable buildings. Large mosque complexes, notably the Yeni Valide mosque and the Sultan Ahmet

The balcony and a column of the Baghdad Pavilion.

OPPOSITE *The columns and terrace wall of the Baghdad Pavilion, built in 1639 after the capture of Baghdad.*

mosque, better known as the Blue Mosque, were raised in the earlier years of the century. Nothing of lasting value was added to Topkapi until the reign of Murad IV, a great warrior and builder, an art lover, poet, and cruel tyrant, who ascended the throne in 1623. Murad restored Ottoman confidence during his ruthless and energetic rule, leading his army in successful campaigns to capture Erivan in Persia and Baghdad. And it was his military achievements, savage, bloody affairs, which were to be commemorated in two of the most charming and intimate pleasure domes to be built anywhere.

Both pavilions, designed by Koca Kasim Aga as meditative retreats, symbolize this period of Ottoman rejuvenation, not on the grand scale of earlier sultans but on a refined personal level, reflecting the private, unhailed aspect of Murad's egotistical nature. The Revan and Baghdad kiosks face each other across a sunken garden in the fourth court, architecturally the most important area of the palace. The less elaborate of the two, the Revan Kiosk, built in 1636 following the Ottoman capture of Erivan, and sometimes referred to as the Turban Room, required the remodelling of an adjacent fountain, one of the original features of the palace built by Mehmet the Conqueror. Within its octagonal walls and projecting iwans (recessed sitting areas), furnished with sofas, Murad, by now addicted to wine, spent days on end accompanied by the new governor of Erivan, toasting, perhaps, the latest Ottoman victory in the east.

For the architect, Kasim Aga, the Revan Kiosk was his first attempt at designing a royal pavilion, and a sign of better things to come. He completed his masterpiece, the Baghdad Kiosk, perched on the northernmost tip of Topkapi Point, just three years later. The interior decor of the kiosk, a single domed building with four symmetrical alcoves, owes much to the legacy of Sinan, the tiling and windows of coloured glass clearly influenced by Murad III's bedroom built sixty years earlier. The same band of calligraphic script, 'The Verse of the Throne', divides the room horizontally, increasing the sense of intimacy in the recessed sitting areas. Richly decorated walls, shimmering as the light catches the glazed Iznik ware, are divided into panels with a refinement that avoids the weakness of excess. Timber shutters and cupboard doors, decorated in geometric patterns of tortoiseshell and mother-of-pearl inlay, contrast with the floral tiles and add to the attraction of the whole.

While Sinan provided a compelling role model it would be wrong to accuse Kasim Aga of designing within the shadow of the true master. Kasim Aga's Baghdad Kiosk is a singular achievement. Unlike Murad III's privy chamber, this is an outdoor room, a summer house, looking outwards as well as within. There are no narrow alleyways leading to its arcaded porch, but a spacious marble terrace. Broad timber eaves, providing shelter from summer sun and showers, cover a two-metre wrap-around gallery with views in three directions. By nature of its design and position it is the ultimate in sultanic pleasure domes.

Murad IV spent little time in his most splendid retreat: he died the year after it was finished. But this area of the fourth court, with its pavilions and marble terrace, clearly pleased his successor Ibrahim, the mad sultan, who presided over one of the most disgraceful reigns in Ottoman history. Soon after ascending to the throne Ibrahim constructed an exquisite gilt-bronze cupola, raised up on four slender piers, in the middle of the terrace balustrade. In Turkish this delicate 'bower' takes its name from the iftar, the evening meal taken after sunset during the month of Ramadan. Ibrahim sat at this beautiful vantage point looking out over the city, waiting for the sun to disappear behind the darkening silhouette of

In the interior of the Baghdad Pavilion, built in 1639, the use of tiled decoration reached its zenith. The building followed the traditional cruciform plan with recessed sitting areas lined with sofas.

the Süleymaniye,the mosque complex of Süleyman the Magnificent, a signal that the day's fast had come to an end.

Ibrahim seems to have had a predilection for spacious terraces. To the north of Topkapi Serai, near the entrance to the Golden Horn, he built the Sepetciler Kiosk, the only summer palace to have survived in what formed part of the seraglio gardens. Distinctly classical, with projecting bays and deep eaves, it is raised up on substantial stone pillars and capped by a slender chimney, typical of those which grace the harem roofscape at Topkapi Palace. To east and west the palace is flanked by elevated terraces where Ottoman sultans used to see off the imperial fleet and welcome its return. Ibrahim also renovated and altered the Circumcision Room, the Sünnet Odasi, which dates back to the reign of Süleyman II, at the southern end of the fourth court terrace. This is most notable for its tiles from various periods taken from dismantled buildings elsewhere and reused. Unintentionally the building illustrates the evolution of Iznik ware.

Ibrahim's most ephemeral contribution to the palace, his huge collection of furs, many imported from Russia, covered the tiled walls and high ceilings of the Baghdad and Revan kiosks and other palace buildings. Excessive expenditure on animal skins, however, contributed to a financial crisis and Ibrahim's political demise. The empire's internal problems grew, corruption was rife amongst tax collectors and other officials, and the treasury was bankrupt. When the Grand Vizier demanded bribes and new furs from the Janissaries to support Ibrahim's obsession and the ailing economy it was the beginning of the end. The Janissaries deposed the madman and imprisoned him in his palace apartments. There he lost his mind and was finally strangled on the orders of the Sheikh-ul-Islam, the chief religious dignitary.

Ibrahim's successor, Mehmet IV, in a long reign that spanned nearly forty years, proved incapable of stemming further decline. Little more than a puppet in the early years of his reign – he was just six years old when he ascended the throne – Mehmet later spent more time hunting and indulging in the pleasures of the harem than attending to the affairs of state. He commissioned few new buildings, limiting himself to essential renovations. After the second major harem fire, which swept through the complex in 1665 when the royal household was away at Edirne, he restored the black eunuchs' dormitories and women's quarters, although the plan remained much as before. Apart from these enforced changes the palace was neglected throughout the latter half of the seventeenth century. Indeed, Mehmet and his three immediate successors spent more time in the old imperial capital at Edirne than they did in Istanbul.

In 1683 the Ottoman army besieged Vienna but were repulsed by Austro-Hungarian forces, signalling a change in Turkish fortunes as Europe went on the offensive. The failure to capture Vienna and further disintegration of the empire opened up a new era in Turco-European relations, paving the way for increasing European influence in the arts and economy of the Ottoman capital. The establishment of agas and senior bureaucrats, increasingly frustrated with the ineffective rule of Mehmet, finally deposed the ruler in 1687. He was 'retired' and sent to live out the rest of his days in a secluded suite at the rear of the harem.

ROCOCO AND TULIPS

The eighteenth century began with the frivolous reign of Sultan Ahmet III and the light-hearted Tulip Period. While Ahmet ignored rising prices, Janissary discontent, conservative opposition to growing western influence and court luxuries, he

A gilded dome, supported on four arches, crowns the interior of the Baghdad Pavilion, designed by the sultan's architect, Kasim Aga. An ornate ball hangs on a long chain from the centre of the ceiling.

ABOVE Ahmet III's Tulip Fountain set into the northern wall of his library sums up the light-heartedness of the Tulip Period and the symbolic importance of water in Islam. Under Ahmet III (1703–30) tulips almost became the icon of the age. They were depicted in fresco panels, in ceramics and carved stone, and Istanbul gardeners eagerly competed with each other to grow the perfect bloom. In spring splendid tulip festivals, preferably illuminated by the light of a full moon, were held in the gardens of the Grand Seraglio.

LEFT The gilded bower, built by Sultan Ibrahim on the terrace of the fourth court, overlooks the Golden Horn and the old city. It was also known as the Iftar Kiosk, after the evening meal which broke the day's fast during the holy month of Ramadan.

lived a civilized lifestyle. In the gardens of Topkapi Serai the annual tulip festival, held on two successive evenings in April, stole the thunder of the traditional religious holidays. In the small garden of the fourth court, between the Baghdad and Revan pavilions, Ahmet planted parterres of tulips. Their colours were mirrored on festival nights, preferably illuminated by a full moon, with lights placed behind glass globes filled with coloured liquids, and the multi-hued costumes of attendants and guests. Additional flickering lights were provided by tortoises which crawled slowly through the tulips with candles waxed to their shells. Slaves danced for the ladies of the harem, poetry recitals and music added to the gaiety of the elegant surroundings. Meanwhile, laughing concubines skipped carefully among the flower beds in search of trinkets and coloured sweets.

The popularity of the tulip soon made it a prominent feature in the tiles and painted decor of Ottoman buildings, inspiring court poets as well as imperial artists. At the beginning of his reign Ahmet redecorated a small room near the harem, the richly painted Fruit Room which represents the quintessence of tulipmania, combined with elements of early Turkish baroque. Arched panels contain vases of flowers, astonishing by their variety and number, arranged with perfect displays of carnations, roses, and irises, as well as tulips. Above a calligraphic band there are bowls of fruit, including fresh green apples; lemons and oranges piled high; and succulent pomegranates revealing delicate pink flesh, bursting with ripeness. This delightful interior is Ahmet's virtuoso performance, an exuberant display designed for pure enjoyment.

In Sultan Ahmet's library, a substantial free-standing building in the centre of the third court, pleasure is combined with learning. Built on the site of an earlier kiosk and pool, the library, although an eighteenth-century structure, is essentially classical with hints of the tulip era. Vases of flowers grace the vault while, on the north façade, decorated with sculptured tulips, stands an attractive wall fountain. On two sides of the building, in a manner reminiscent of the fifteenth-century Tiled Kiosk, steps lead to a raised entrance beneath a substantial porch. Within, the library is flooded with natural light. The upper windows, similar to those in the Baghdad Kiosk but with a greater area of glass, and translucent rather than coloured, illuminate the domed interior and the reading bays where users sat cross-legged in front of books and manuscripts placed on wooden stands. The library was open regularly on Mondays and Wednesdays and readers could borrow books, stored in recessed cupboards, on the proviso that they remained within the palace walls.

If Ahmet's library praised the virtues of scholarly pursuit, his greatest imperial monument, the street fountain near the palace's Imperial Gate, was built in worship of water. With this fine example of Turkish rococo architecture Ahmet began the fashion for free-standing fountains, building on the tradition of wall fountains as neighbourhood and wayside meeting-places. Ahmet built no mosque; flower festivals, books, and poetry were his priorities. Water, however, remained an important symbol of Islam. And in a city which has always suffered from problems of water supply, a huge, ornate fountain was an appropriate structure with which to commemorate his reign.

The building's walls, richly ornamented and vying for attention, provide a canvas for the surface tiling, patterns of fruit and flowers, calligraphic panels, and sculptured niches. Gently curving corners, so typical of rococo design, pick up the line of the deep eaves. At each corner, semi-circular sebils, part of the larger monumental fountain, have ornate bronze grilles, and reach up visually through the roof, capped by four turrets with gilded finials. A larger fifth turret crowns the

Built and decorated in 1706, during the illustrious Tulip Period, Ahmet III's Fruit Room or dining-room, with its exuberant displays of painted flowers and fruit bursting with ripeness.

apex. Beautiful and self-glorifying, Ahmet's fountain displays his own chrono-grammatic verse (the numerical values of the letters giving the date of erection): 'Drink the water and say a prayer for Sultan Ahmet.' Other inscriptions, in gold letters on a blue-green background, written by the celebrated poet Seyyid Vehbi, praise the fountain and its creator in twenty-seven verses.

In addition to the new buildings at Topkapi Serai, Ahmet built a large new pleasure palace, Sa'dabat, 'The Palace of Happiness', at the tip of the Golden Horn, in an area popularly referred to as the 'Sweet Waters of Europe'. Sa'dabat, de-signed in a style intended to emulate the French royal palaces, heralded the begin-ning of European influence in Ottoman architecture as leading officials began to accept new ideas from abroad. The first Ottoman ambassador to France, Yirmisekiz Çelebi Mehmet Efendi, was appointed to Paris in 1720 and instructed to visit French fortresses, factories, palaces, and other buildings which could be adapted to suit the Ottoman empire. Yirmisekiz Çelebi was particularly attracted by the lifestyle of Louis XV. He brought back plans and sketches of Versailles and Fontainebleau, pleasing the Grand Vizier, Ibrahim Pasha, who believed that a good knowledge of Europe was important for the development of Ottoman foreign policy. Ibrahim himself supervised the construction of Sa'dabat, a poor imitation of Versailles surrounded by baths, statues, fountains and gardens. 'The Palace of Happiness' had none of the permanence of French architecture: the monumental formality of Versailles, which took fifty years to complete, was married to the Turkish tradition of a temporary royal encampment of tents. Nearly 200 pavilions of lath and plaster were clustered around courtyards where orange trees bloomed, a present from the French ambassador, the Marquis de Villeneuve.

Sa'dabat itself formed a model for smaller private palaces and pavilions which were to spring up throughout Istanbul. There was a new appreciation of nature and fresh air; old artistic traditions, such as the ban on representing the human form, were relaxed; and the first printing press for Ottoman Turkish, devised by a Hungarian convert, printed a map of the Marmara Sea in 1720, followed by geo-graphical and historical works. Turkish diplomats in Paris, including Yirmisekiz Çelebi's son, the first Ottoman to have a fair grasp of French, brought European furniture, books, and costumes back to Istanbul. These soon gained an exotic appeal among wealthy Turks, creating a significant demand for European goods.

As well as the attractions of Europe, Sultan Ahmet cheerfully promoted the work of Ottoman poets who caught the spirit and pleasure of the tulip age. Litera-ture broke new ground, casting off the influence of the east and creating a pure Ottoman literature, before the adoption of European ways began to affect the written word. Foremost among the new era Divan poets, Ahmet Nedim, founder of the naturalist school which prevailed throughout the eighteenth century, spent long periods entertaining the sultan at Sa'dabat and at another new palace at Çirağan.

Poetic appreciation and the enjoyment of spring festivals, however, are not sufficient qualities on which to base the rule of a struggling empire. After surren-dering territory to the 'infidel' Shia Muslims in Iran, Ahmet III was overthrown by disgruntled army officers in 1830 and his flimsy pleasure domes at Sa'dabat were wantonly destroyed. Thus came to an end the frivolous, yet in many ways one of the most enlightened reigns of the Ottoman dynasty.

As the eighteenth century progressed the floral designs of the tulip era were abandoned and architects fully embraced rococo rhetoric, in the process sealing the fate of classical Ottoman architecture. Mahmut I proved to be less reactionary than the Janissary rebels had hoped, continuing with the cultural development and

Detail of the walls of Ahmet III's Fruit Room.

During his twenty-seven-year reign in the early eighteenth century, Ahmet III began the fashion for free-standing street fountains. Nothing has been built since to compete with his huge rococo structure outside the seraglio's Imperial Gate, inscribed with a chronogrammatic verse: 'Drink the water and say a prayer for Sultan Ahmet.'

The library of Ahmet III in the third courtyard. Most of the books were moved to the 'new library', the former mosque of the Palace School. Among its 5000 volumes are Korans transcribed by successive Caliphs and the only original Greek account of the fall of Constantinople, written by the historian Critoboulus.

Osman III's kiosk, the last addition at Topkapi Palace to significantly alter its skyline, included two major influences. The western wing, pictured here, perched above the palace walls, was based on the vernacular tradition of projecting cumbas, or bay windows. The interior and eastern façade, however, reflected the rococo fashion of the eighteenth century.

The Sofa Kiosk, refurbished with a lively rococo interior in 1752, contains a gilded brazier presented to the court by Louis XV.

reform begun under Ahmet III. At Topkapi the gradual merging of European and Ottoman taste is best illustrated by the Sofa Kiosk, refurbished in 1752 and the gayest rococo interior in the palace. A glass pavilion framed in wood, the kiosk's principal room is raised a full storey above ground level on slim marble columns. The fusion of two cultures is most successfully achieved in the light-filled interior where a fine example of a rococo brazier, made by Jean-Claude Duplessis the elder, fits comfortably into the Euro-Ottoman room. One of a pair, the gilded brazier was a gift to the Ottoman ambassador from Louis XV.

The free-flowing lines of rococo clearly suited the Ottoman temperament. During the latter half of the eighteenth century there was barely a sultan who could resist building his own ornate private room, within or adjacent to the harem. Osman III, in a brief three-year reign during the 1750s, added several substantial buildings, although he appears not to have cared for the other arts. At Topkapi, his exquisite wooden kiosk, one of the last additions to affect the palace skyline, picks up the rococo language and marries it firmly with the vernacular tradition. Built adjacent to an elevated garden, the western arm of the salon, supported on a large wooden corbel, juts out high above the harem walls, reflecting the large town houses or wooden yalis along the Bosphorus. The eastern façade and interior, however, have clear rococo traits. The ceiling, decorated with wooden rococo mouldings, meets the stuccoed wall, set with blue and white Delft tiles and wood veneer surrounds.

The kiosks of both Mahmut I and Osman III exhibit a certain decorative restraint, but later sultans were to project the exuberance of the baroque in all its gilded magnificence. Turkish baroque reached its peak in such interiors as the hall of the Mihrisah Sultane Valide; the Chamber of Abdul Hamid I; and Selim III's salon where twists and curls of gilded wood, golden fronds and fluid vegetal forms, mirrors and tile panels, fuse in the dream-like state of rococo enchantment. In Selim III's salon, a glittering room blended from Islamic and European elements, stands a wall fountain decorated with scalloped shells. On the walls, frescos of imaginary landscapes, probably painted by European artists, complete the flamboyant fantasy world, an invigorating substitute for an outside world largely unseen.

Ancillary palaces built or adopted during the period of baroque experimentation have all disappeared except for the substantial Aynalikavak Pavilion, the only surviving part of a complex originally known as the Tersane, or 'Dockyard', Palace on the northern banks of the Golden Horn. Situated among fine gardens dominated by cedars and magnolias, the pavilion was originally built during the reign of Ahmet III (1703–30). Early eighteenth-century miniatures depict a timber structure with trellised windows and, in the foreground, celebrations for the circumcision of Ahmet III's sons. The pavilion was later remodelled under Selim III, who retained the central cupola but refurbished the interior with rococo embellishments. The principal Royal Audience Chamber is lit with panelled windows of coloured glass; and the walls are decorated with gilded tracery, scallops, and scrollwork, monograms of Selim III and gold calligraphic inscriptions on a deep blue ground. The frail fabric covering the couch in the music-room dates back to Selim's time and the floor is still carpeted in the original reed matting. The pavilion takes its name, literally the 'Mirrored Poplar' pavilion, from large gilded mirrors, presents to Ahmet III from the Venetians, that were hung here. It also gave its name to the Aynalikavak Treaty, signed in 1784, which conceded Russian annexation of the Crimea and allowed Catherine the Great to establish a foothold along the Black Sea coast.

The Imperial Hall or Royal Salon is the largest room in the palace. Dating back to the sixteenth century, it was rebuilt after a disastrous fire in 1665 and redecorated a century later. While the sultan reclined on the canopied throne, male musicians were sometimes brought, blindfolded, to entertain the harem ladies.

The Composition Room, a side-room of the *Aynalikavak Pavilion*, where Selim III is believed to have composed much of his music.

The Ottoman interpretation of the baroque, represented by Selim's pavilion and his salon at Topkapi Palace, successfully projected a distinctness of its own, a true fusion of styles, but as Turkey entered the nineteenth century cultural dilution began to settle in. Turkish architects, notably the Balian family, responsible for most of the nineteenth-century palaces which sprang up along the Bosphorus, became chained to a personal interpretation of western classicism, effectively bringing to an end a native style. At Topkapi there was an exception to the embracement of the west; a splendid onion-domed kiosk reconstructed during the reign of Mahmut II (1808–39). This, the Alay Kiosk, perched atop a strategic corner of the palace's outer wall, was built on the site of a much earlier review pavilion where sultans watched passing guild processions through latticed windows.

Window detail of the baroque Throne Room.

Many bloody stories, captivating if exaggerated, have been told about the Alay Kiosk. The tyrannical Murad IV allegedly used it to practise his archery skills on passers-by. After public grumbling about the sultan's latest sickening pastime he limited himself to ten heads per shoot. During the 1655 Janissary revolt, Mehmet IV saved his own skin by hurling the bodies of his Chief Black and White Eunuchs to the angry crowd, followed by most of his principal ministers the following day. In more peaceful times it was more commonly a meeting-place for the sultan and his entourage prior to Friday prayers at the mosque. But its chief function as a viewing pavilion allowed the sultan to admire the commercial dynamism of his growing city. Grand review parades continued until the end of the eighteenth century.

One of the greatest processions, held in 1638, was witnessed by Evliya Çelebi whose father served as chief gold-maker in the palace. That year, Murad IV ordered city dignitaries, guild leaders, and imams to prepare an inventory of Constantinople that was to be kept in the administrative offices of the Sublime Porte. All the mosques and mesjids; schools, colleges, and convents; caravanserais, hans, baths, and fountains; places of worship, the churches, and synagogues; houses, gardens, and yalis; even ovens and windmills were included. Nothing was to be left out. The inventory took three months to complete, after which a boisterous procession of the guilds passed below the Alay Kiosk.

There were hundreds of guilds, although Çelebi's figure of a thousand and one appears exaggerated. At the procession silver-threadmakers, blacksmiths, saddlers, and feltmakers displayed the products of their trade. Animal trainers, beating the tambourine, encouraged their bears to dance for the sultan. Firework-makers, of which there were a round hundred, lit up the skies. 'On the occasions of rejoicing for victories,' wrote Çelebi, 'these firework-makers set on fire some hundred thousand rockets of different colours, some of which mount straight into the sky, and some go in an oblique direction, spreading stars around them.' Then came the fools and mimics; the flower-sellers, throwing fruit and fresh blooms to the crowd; and the scent merchants, sprinkling spectators with frankincense and rose-water. Less attractive were the executioners and the tools of their grisly trade: sharpened swords, nails, razors, and 'different powders for blinding, clubs for breaking the hands and feet . . .' Like the other guilds the executioners were protected by their patron saint, Job, the first to cut off the head of a murderer.

The polygonal Alay Kiosk, solid, with deep overhanging eaves, is one of the last examples of the baroque, even if it is not so easy to categorize as the top-heavy entrance to the Sublime Porte opposite, completed a couple of years later. The exuberance of Selim III's salon is here replaced with a lightness of touch. Painted urns overflowing with sinuous foliage, and wreaths linked with a key-like pattern,

The baroque Throne Room or Royal Audience Chamber at Aynalikavak Pavilion, the only surviving building of the Tersane ('Dockyard') Palace on the northern banks of the Golden Horn. Although the palace dates back to the reign of Ahmet III, it was remodelled by Selim III (1789–1807), who refurbished the interior with baroque and rococo embellishments.

Details of the walls in the
Throne Rom of *Aynalikavak*
Pavilion.

decorate the internal walls. The shell-like forms of Selim's fireplace reappear in an unexpected place; as a functional basin in the sultan's toilet.

The Alay Kiosk is a far more appropriate building for Topkapi Point than the last pavilion to be built there, the incongruous Abdul Mecit Kiosk. Modelled on the sultan's ideas about the latest fashions in French court architecture, it is distinctly foreign in its setting in the fourth court. It lies at the extremity of Topkapi Point, looking out and along the shores of the Bosphorus where Abdul Mecit's quest for European-influenced 'modernity' was finally to lead him.

3

---------- ⁂ ----------

WOODEN MANSIONS

Each villa on the Bosphorus looks a screen
New painted, or a pretty opera-scene.

Lord Byron

The villas which captivated Byron during his visit to Istanbul in the early nineteenth century were the grand wooden houses, known as yalis, perched on the waterfront as summer retreats from the bustling centre of the old city. From the end of the seventeenth century onwards leading pashas and grand viziers raised their waterside residences along the Bosphorus, against a green backdrop of forested hillsides and, in spring, the fiery bloom of the Judas trees. Built for pleasure and prestige, many yalis were added to as the owners' requirements changed. Additional wings were raised on timber piles and new bays projected over the sea.

Ottoman yalis passed through several distinct phases as the city adapted to new ideas largely imported from abroad. In their original form they were perched on the water's edge – the name is derived from the Greek *yialos*, 'seashore' – with cantilevered *cumbas*, or bay windows, jutting out over the water. Within, pashas and their entourages sat in recessed sitting areas lined with velvet-covered divans. The projecting bays and deep overhanging eaves created a strong pattern of light and shade on the wooden façades. Roofs were tiled and walls painted a characteristic terracotta red, sometimes known as 'Ottoman Rose'. It was an understated architectural form, based largely on the vernacular tradition, which belied the exotic interiors within, where fountains cooled the summer heat and flower paintings covered the walls. In these palatial homes distant Shamanistic influences, derived from the Turkic homelands in central Asia, were meshed with the requirements of Islam, with the demands of a moist maritime climate, and with the decorative arts of Persia.

As the eighteenth century progressed the traditional interiors became embellished with rococo appliqué. The plan and exterior changed little, but scallops and foliate decorations were introduced above the windows and doors in increasingly theatrical interiors. Trompe-l'œil effects presented illusionistic Bosphorus scenes, and several of the grander yalis had domed ceilings representing the traditional nomadic tent.

The baroque, however, was soon to give way to a cosmopolitan eclecticism which reached its peak in the second half of the nineteenth century, at the same time that the Balian family of architects were building their imposing Euro-palaces for sultans Abdul Mecit and Abdul Aziz. During this period the yali concept underwent radical change. Instead of being sited on the water's edge, the homes were

The first-floor study of the eighteenth-century Fethi Ahmet Pasha yali, raised up on slender timber columns. The idea of elevated architecture impressed Le Corbusier when he visited Constantinople in 1911 and ultimately led to his monumental buildings, such as the Unité d'Habitation in Marseilles, supported on gigantic concrete pilotis.

OVERLEAF *At the beginning of the twentieth century the romantic French writer Pierre Loti, author of Suprêmes Visions d'Orient, was a frequent guest in the yali of Count Ostrorog, legal adviser to the Sublime Porte.*

RIGHT The Köprülü Amcazâde Hüseyin Pasha yali, built in 1698, is the oldest waterfront mansion still standing. As well as being a classic Ottoman yali, it has been witness to far-reaching historical events. In 1699 the Turco-Austrian Karlowitz Treaty, which marked the transition of the Ottoman Empire from an expanding power to its gradual descent into the role of 'sick man of Europe', was ratified here.

OPPOSITE ABOVE Windows and shutters of the Ethem Perter yali at Kanlica.

OPPOSITE BELOW Roof detail of Hekimbaşilarin yali: deep overhanging eaves were characteristic of early yalis.

BELOW The eighteenth-century Hekimbaşilarin yali at Kandilli on the Asian shore. Early yalis were traditionally painted rust-red or 'Ottoman rose' before lighter pastel shades were introduced through increasing contacts with Europe.

pushed back behind a narrow quay. They were painted a variety of colours, creams, pinks, and lemon, as well as the traditional reddish-brown; and Turkish vernacular forms gave way to houses based on a variety of European models. Italianate villas and elaborate mansions with 'gothic' towers and onion domes reflected the uneasy eclecticism of the nineteenth century.

Most wealthy Turks had their seasonal houses on the edge of the straits, but they retained their winter konak, or town house, in the city. Each summer the whole family moved up the Bosphorus, rowed along the forested shore in their wooden caiques. Others left Istanbul for resorts along the Marmara coast or to spend the summer on one of the nearby Princes' Islands.

It is a pattern of life which, to some extent, is still adhered to today. Several owners of the larger, older yalis now live abroad, returning to the Bosphorus for a long summer vacation. Most continue to keep their winter residence in town, spending the summer, as well as fine spring and autumn weekends, on the waterfront. But with the improvement in communications the yalis are now no great distance from the centres of economic life, culture, and commerce and some are lived in all year round.

ASIAN ORIGINS

The origins of the Turkish yali can be traced back to the nomadic Turkic tribes which roamed an area that today forms part of Outer Mongolia, south of the Yenisei River and east of the Eurasian steppelands. Their mobile civilization had no formal government but was based on tribal customs, the raising of animals, and the search for fresh pastures in the Altai Mountains. They were Shamanists who worshipped the elements and nature spirits through totem symbols believed to have special powers over mankind. From the second century BC, following changed climatic and political conditions in the Altai homeland, successive waves of nomads moved south and west towards the Middle East and Europe where, in lands where they chose to remain, they supplanted more static communities.

Some settled along the borders of the Middle East where the influence of the Muslim empires of Iran and Iraq resulted in the formation of the Göktürk Empire, the first Turkish political union. Extending from the Black Sea, through Asia, along Mongolia's northern borders and into China, it lasted from AD 552 to 744 before breaking up into its constituent tribes. Among those who continued to dominate the Transoxiana territories after the collapse of the empire were the Uygurs who lived in the upper basin of the Yenisei River from 745 until displaced by the Kirghiz in the mid-ninth century. While most tribes continued to live in felt tents it was the Uygurs who are believed to have been among the first to develop a rudimentary plan for the Turkish house.

The Uygurs and adjacent tribes continued to practise Shamanistic rites but were also influenced by Buddhist missionaries from China and, as a result, began to adopt a more settled existence. Uygur architecture appears to have been determined by a mix of Shamanistic belief and Buddhist cosmology. According to Shamanistic tradition the supreme Being was placed on a mountain of gold located on an octagonal island; while Buddhist symbolism interpreted the world as a square plateau floating in the celestial ocean. This fusion of ancient beliefs led to buildings oriented according to the four cardinal compass points and based on a cross-axial or cruciform plan. One Uygur text develops the idea of floor plans based on cosmographic principles and suggests that inhabitants move from room

The eighteenth-century Zarif Mustafa Pasha yali on the Asian shore was badly damaged recently when a ship rammed its seafront façade. Impenetrable fog and strong Bosphorus currents are major navigational hazards.

OVERLEAF Named after a Cyprus-born Grand Vizier to Sultan Mahmut II, the Kibrisli yali, one of the largest of the waterfront mansions, has been in the same family for seven generations.

to room according to the seasons. The importance of intermediate points between the cardinal directions led to octagonal buildings. Some rooms imitated the form of the domed tent, and the Uygurs built Chinese-style kiosks in painted wood.

Other cruciform timber structures with truncated internal corners were raised on a square podium. The principal façades contained openings functioning as windows and doors, covered with shutters of wickerwork or reeds. Internal walls of cob, a mixture of clay, gravel, and straw, were decorated in polychrome designs and, in each of the truncated corners, niches contained ritualistic statues. At the centre of the home, smoke drifted from a brazier and escaped through an opening in the roof.

If the Uygurs were the first to establish a pattern or basis for the Turkish house it was their successors who were to carry it westwards. During the tenth century the powerful Seljuks, converts to Islam, entered the Middle East and became protectors of the societies they had conquered. While Turkish civilization as a whole adopted the religion of Muhammad, the character of their houses changed little except that figurative statues, forbidden by the new religion, disappeared.

As Seljuk power began to wane in the thirteenth century the more powerful and successful Ottomans rose to take their place. They expanded Turkish suzerainty further west into the Balkans and southwards into Arab lands, and in 1453 they captured Constantinople, the jewel in the Ottoman crown. There the tradition of Turkish timber construction was to reach its apogee in the grand seventeenth- and eighteenth-century yalis on the Bosphorus.

Between the rudimentary structures of central Asia and the sophisticated Bosphorus yalis, transitional buildings once graced the meadows of the Golden Horn at Kâğithane and the royal palace at Edirne where many of the garden pavilions – the 'Nightingale', 'Tent', and 'Hunt' kiosks – were built of timber on stone bases. The plan of the sea-front yalis is also related to the fifteenth-century Çinili Kiosk and the later Baghdad Pavilion at Topkapi Serai, as well as some larger provincial konaks, where the cruciform plan was often skewed to adapt to tight urban sites. Old symbolism sometimes resulted in a sky-blue ceiling or central dome, with similar-sized rooms painted in different colours. The cross-shaped plan remained important in domestic Ottoman architecture until the nineteenth century, but whether the symbolism retained any real meaning for the inhabitants, or whether the plans were simply adopted from earlier models, is open to conjecture.

If the plan of Çinili Kiosk influenced waterfront houses, the layout of the yalis is also analogous to the courtyard principal at Topkapi Palace. The large central hallway, the sofa, was the public space; the inner courtyard was where family members held receptions and socialized in groups. Leading from the sofa were small private rooms, analogous to the serai's kiosks and pavilions, where pashas retired to study state papers or for their evening rest.

The plans of the earliest yalis certainly stirred the romantic imagination of Ahmet Nedim, a Tulip Period poet and companion of Ahmet III. He likened the twin-winged yalis to a bird in flight:

> The onlooker, seeing this façade . . .
> Thinks of a phoenix with open wings . . .

Nedim, whose work echoed the nature-loving spirit of the times, also referred to four early yalis in a series of chronogrammatic poems:

> Loftily rose Mustafa Pasha's sea-side mansion,
> . . . (a) delicately ornate castle on the sea.

ABOVE Detail of the façade of the Kibrisli yali.

BELOW The grand central sofa of the Kibrisli yali, built in 1775, follows the traditional cruciform plan with four corner rooms. The hall runs the full width of the house with windows overlooking the Bosphorus on one side; the garden is on the other.

MUSIC BY MOONLIGHT

The Grand Vizier Kibrisli Mehmet Pasha bought the Kibrisli yali in 1840. His wife, Melek Hanum, wrote one of the most reliable accounts of women's life in an upper-class household, Thirty Years in the Harem, *published in 1872.*

OPPOSITE *The winter garden with its marble fountain and intricate pebble floor, decorated in a style that was inherited from the Byzantines.*

Nedim's 'delicately ornate castles' underwent considerable change during the nineteenth century, but waterside living lost none of its irresistible lure. Towards the end of the century the Bosphorus witnessed celebrations the like of which had not been seen since the Tulip Period. Among the highlights of the social calendar, and some of the most attractive of Ottoman entertainments, were the summer *mehtab*, or moonlight concerts. For a perfect concert, with music drifting from shore to shore, conditions had to be just right; the Bosphorus relatively calm, the moon full and shining down through a cloudless sky. Concerts were thus limited to three or four each summer, with no more than one procession allowed on any one night.

Towards the end of the century, when the number of yalis had reached its peak, hundreds of boats followed each other on *mehtab* nights from the southern entrance of the straits to the calm bay at Bebek. The procession was led by the concert boat, a specially adapted caique with a raised deck for the musicians and singers. In the women's caiques ladies sat wrapped in silk cloaks and veiled in white yashmaks. From the stern of the boats they trailed pieces of velvet or satin, 'embroidered in gold or silver and edged with little silver fishes, (which) floated on the waves' as described by the chronicler Emine Foat Tugay. Before the evening's entertainment the musicians were traditionally received in the yalis of the leading dignitaries who were mounting the event. At the beginning of the twentieth century, hosts were as varied as Sait Halim Pasha, an Egyptian prince and Grand Vizier whose house at Yeniköy remains one of the best preserved of nineteenth-century yalis; Sami Bey, a celebrated socialite; and the mother of the last Khedive of Egypt, Abbas Hilmi II.

As the procession wove its way between the Bosphorus currents musicians played instrumental pieces on violins, lutes, and dulcimers, interspersed with melancholy love songs. Caiques crossed from shore to shore calling at yalis belonging to the host's relatives and stopping at particularly notable homes. From the windows of the yalis onlookers, silhouetted by candlelight, gazed out at the extraordinary spectacle. In the normally quiet villages young and old crowded along the shoreline, eager for a glimpse of the floating orchestra.

Second only to the moonlit concerts for sheer delight were the regular illuminations which were best appreciated on a gentle cruise after sunset. On the sultan's birthday small lamps lit up the gardens and façades of the imperial palaces and larger yalis, and gardens were opened to the public. The shores were also gaily lit on the Prophet's birthday, when sweets were distributed in silk and satin bags decorated with floral motifs, stitched by ladies of the harem. Dolmabahçe Palace is still occasionally illuminated on republic day and other important state occasions, reminding the water-borne commuter, perhaps, of how life was lived in more heady days.

As well as palatial retreats yalis were centres of political intrigue where plots were hatched and treaties signed. Several of the most far-reaching accords in Ottoman history were signed or ratified in the Köprülü yali, the oldest yali still in existence. And at Sait Halim Pasha's yali at Yeniköy, Sultan Abdul Hamid's secret agents were frequent and unwelcome visitors.

The notorious spy Kim Philby also lived in a yali at Beylerbey after taking up a post as First Secretary with the British Embassy in 1947. Under diplomatic cover he

OPPOSITE ABOVE Built high above the Bosphorus shore, the Çürüksulu Ahmet Pasha yali near Üsküdar commands magnificent views of the old city and its dramatic skyline of Topkapi Palace, Haghia Sophia, and the Sultan Ahmet mosque.

OPPOSITE BELOW The eighteenth-century yali is the only one of four houses once attached to the large Salacak Palace to have survived.

LEFT The luscious garden encroaches on the Çürüksulu Ahmet Pasha yali.

was sent to spy for the Secret Intelligence Services, although his real employers were the KGB. Philby's life on the Asiatic shore was livened up during visits by his fellow-spy Guy Burgess who, after several drinks too many, took to plunging into the Bosphorus from the upper floor of the yali and swimming back to the shore.

Other foreigners of less dubious repute invariably admired Istanbul's waterside houses. 'Nothing can be more irregular, and consequently more picturesque, than the style of building on the Bosphorus,' wrote Julia Pardoe in 1836. Le Corbusier described the Turkish house as 'an architectural masterpiece'. He was impressed by the way in which rooms were cantilevered over the water and took particular note of the remarkable first floor wings at the eighteenth-century Mocan yali which are raised on tall timber columns.

Abdullah Şinasi Hisar, one of Turkey's leading authors of the early twentieth century, portrayed the latter period of Ottoman decline through the eyes of the upper classes. In a book about his childhood before the First World War, he described days of lazy abandon when groups of men and women rowed along the Bosphorus in separate caiques, passed the yalis, and stopped at Küçüksu Palace to admire the view. 'The yalis, kayiks, even the ladies, formed a pattern, appearing each in its proper place.' Hisar once spotted the incurable romantic Pierre Loti wearing a fez and seated in a caique with two pairs of rowers.

But it was not just wealthy Ottomans and adoptive Turks, such as Loti, who were able to enjoy the Bosphorus and its shoreline. Each summer European diplomats and businessmen, eager to escape the city heat, rented rooms or houses in the coastal villages. In 1910, the poet James Elroy Flecker, author of *Hassan* and *The Golden Journey to Samarkand*, was appointed to the British consulate in Istanbul. Along with other junior officers he spent the summer at Kandilli on the Asian shore where he described the 'terrible and malignant beauty' of the Bosphorus. In these surroundings he understood 'why men of the East will sit by a fountain from noon to night, and let the world roll onward.' Like Hisar, Flecker caught sight of Pierre Loti who also passed some of his time at Kandilli. He seemed unimpressed, noting that the novelist, then into his sixties, painted himself to look young.

As early as the 1720s, as the Turkish chronicler Küçük Çelebizâde Asim Efendi observed, the yalis' traditional terracotta red was beginning to give way to pastel shades introduced under the influence of Europe. Different communities in the city could often be identified by the colour of their homes. Along the Bosphorus, Turks, Armenians, and Greeks lived in separate villages, rarely meeting each other except for business. The Turks' houses were painted in fanciful, gay colours prohibited to other groups. Armenians confined themselves to red; the Greeks, to a lead colour; while the Jews, descendants of the Sephardic community expelled from Spain in 1492, were compelled to colour their houses black. Some of the Porte's wealthiest ministers and businessmen painted their spacious homes in two distinct colours, giving the effect of separate but attached dwellings.

HAREMS AND HAMAMS

In principal yalis, as in the imperial palaces, there was a strict separation of apartments for the men and women of the household – the selamlik and harem. Even the husband and wife took their meals separately and received their guests in their own apartments. Meals were cooked in an outbuilding, where copper pans and earthenware pots simmered over charcoal fires fanned, as one traveller noted, 'by a negress cook with a turkey's wing'.

In common with other houses, one of the Çürüksulu yali's principal rooms, now used as a dining-room, runs the entire depth of the house. The timber ceiling is centred on a carved cabbage, salvaged from another Ottoman house.

OPPOSITE The library, assembled by the yali's previous owner, the late Turkish diplomat Muharrem Nuri Birgi. During the 1970s and early 80s Mr Birgi patiently restored the dilapidated yali which now houses his eclectic collection of art and antiques, comprising Chinese paintings, imperial Ottoman decrees, rare books, Turkish daggers, blue-and-white ware from Canton.

LEFT Rose-water sprinklers, popular throughout the Middle East, were produced in the Beykoz factory on the Asian shore of the Bosphorus where glass manufacture probably began during the reign of Selim III (1789–1807). Genuine Beykoz ware, however, is often difficult to distinguish from Bohemian sprinklers made for the oriental market.

...e eighteenth-century stairway with carved banisters and ...alcony containing a small shelf.

In a first-floor sitting-room Chinese paintings, bought in Peking, hang on the wall. The room is furnished with fake Louis XVI chairs and cabinets manufactured in Istanbul towards the end of the nineteenth century.

Sometimes the harem and selamlik were two separate buildings with gardens or a courtyard in between. To screen the women, who were forbidden to appear in public without a veil, windows were protected from outside viewers by wooden grilles which slid up and down in grooved channels. Within, these modesty screens, known appropriately as 'jalousies', subdued the light, adding to the intimate atmosphere, and allowing women to watch the world go by without themselves being seen.

Turkish men could have several wives – and sultans certainly did – but most were content with one. The harem, far from being a den of debauchery, was primarily the preserve of the female members of the family; mothers, aunts, stepmothers, cousins, sisters, and female friends whose husbands were abroad attending to affairs of state. One of the most reliable sources about life in an upper-class harem is the 1872 autobiography of Melek Hanum who spent thirty years in different harems and stayed with friends while her husband was ambassador to London. For her harem life was often enjoyable: 'We passed the time very pleasantly together, in conversation, dancing, music, listening to and telling stories; in fact, seeking to entertain ourselves in every way we could imagine.' Once she complained of the 'tedious routine of harem life' but this was relieved by visiting ladies and eunuchs from the sultan's court. Leading harems, although not the imperial harem, often held the equivalent of today's coffee mornings, when twenty to thirty women would gather to exchange gossip, smoke, and drink coffee or sherbet.

Houses were built for large, extended families. Sons brought their wives and children to the harem under the ever watchful eye of the senior lady, usually the grandmother, who reigned supreme over all domestic matters. By the beginning of the twentieth century the distinction between harem and selamlik began to disappear, the speed of change dependent on the outlook of the ageing matriarch. The selamlik and its adjacent gardens increasingly became used for cocktails and garden parties to which women were welcome, if not equal, guests.

The main room of each yali, the central sofa, with rooms opening off it on all four sides, was designed to make full use of the changing light and a seafront setting. On hot summer days, isolated from the heat by peripheral rooms and with one or two fountains to help freshen the heavy seasonal air, it was the coolest place in the house. As well as central free-standing fountains set in an octagonal or circular pool there were wall-mounted, musical fountains known as *şelsebils*. These were usually found in yali gardens, although a fine pair, still in working order, play a stereophonic tune in the downstairs sofa of the Mocan yali at Kuzguncuk. *Şelsebils* consist of carved marble panels with projecting 'cups' positioned so that water trickles down from one to another. It was also common for one of the house's principal façades to contain a double row of windows, the upper one glazed with stained glass, adding a touch of coloured light to the spacious interior.

The sofa contained little furniture, free-standing chairs, tables, and sideboards only being introduced as the Turks' taste for European goods grew during the nineteenth century. The only obligatory fitting was the *sedir*, a large, low divan for sitting and reclining fixed at the head of the room. Oriental carpets from Turkey, Persia, and central Asia covered the floor and cushions were scattered on the divan. Bedding was rolled up during the day and squeezed into fitted cupboards.

Family treasures, collections of copperware, porcelain, glass, and gems, were stored away in chests, along with the ladies' brocades, silks, and embroideries. 'Were they displayed in the reception rooms (they) would add greatly to the cheerfulness of their appearance,' observed Lucy Garnett as late as 1904. 'But this is

not the practice of the Osmanlis, who retain in many of their habits the characteristics of their nomadic ancestors.'

Often a huge *mangal*, a charcoal brazier of copper or brass, stood in the centre of the room. While this was rarely used in yalis solely inhabited during the summer, it took the chill off cool evenings at the beginning and end of each season. An old-fashioned *mangal* still stands in the eighteenth-century Kibrisli yali, one of the largest of the early houses, currently being restored by a family which has lived there for seven generations. No form of modern heating has been installed, but in an exquisite glass-panelled room, known as the winter garden, a brazier warms the air, scented with the fragrance of rose-petals.

Another form of heating was provided by the *tandir*, literally 'oven', a sort of table made of deal, with a lower shelf lined in tin. A pan of burning charcoal was placed in the centre and the whole contraption covered with a thickly padded quilt. Seated on divans to each side, members of the family pulled the edge of the quilt over their knees, drawing warmth from the glowing embers. The *tandir* was a potentially dangerous form of heating, particularly when younger members of the household gathered to share its warmth. 'When the circle is composed of young girls, they become extremely animated, tease each other, throw fruit and nuts, and excite themselves by playful interchanges of kicks and blows,' explained Melek Hanum. 'This kind of entertainment is sometimes attended with serious results, as the foot-warmer occasionally gets overturned, and sets fire to the house.'

For most Ottoman ladies regular trips to the neighbourhood hamam was a highlight of the week. Women usually went in groups, taking the younger children, including boys, with them, and shuffled about the steamy interior in raised clogs inlaid with mother-of-pearl. Baths were invariably domed with small windows in the roof and divided into the dressing, tepid, and steam rooms. The most luxurious were paved with marble and covered with cushions and carpets. The hamam was an important social centre where women eagerly exchanged neighbourhood and family news. Among the upper classes, however, many felt the public baths, however luxurious, were unsuitable for them and they confined their bathing to the family hamam.

Most of the larger yalis had their own Turkish bath, usually a separate and free-standing building. Maintaining a regular temperature in private baths was more difficult than in the busy neighbourhood baths in daily use, but this was a minor inconvenience, compensated for in terms of social standing. In the privacy of their own hamams Ottoman ladies were attended by young slave girls who vigorously scrubbed their mistresses' bodies with serge cloths, tinted their nails with henna, and braided their hair. This image of the Ottoman hamam, often romanticized by European artists such as Jean-Léon Gérôme, is now quaint and obsolete. Neighbourhood baths can still be found in some of the poorer and older areas of Istanbul, but the private hamam was ousted by the western-style bathroom several generations ago.

TULIPS AND TREATIES

Of the few early wooden yalis that survive the Köprülü Amcazâde Hüseyin Pasha yali, built in 1698, has one of the most interesting and well documented histories. Architecturally the yali belongs to the delightful Tulip Period, with hints of Persian influence. At the turn of the twentieth century the large two-storey harem, its upper windows decorated with stained glass, was demolished leaving only the

Upstairs living-room of Fethi Ahmet Pasha yali.

OPPOSITE Probably designed by a Venetian architect, the grand double staircase, its banisters shaped like harps, was influenced by the baroque.

ABOVE LEFT Detail of banisters.

ABOVE RIGHT A wall fountain and Kütahya tiles in the central sofa. Two fountains with baroque-like scallops, are set into opposite walls and still play their liquid tunes.

LEFT The central oblong hall lies parallel to the Bosphorus yet, unusually, has no windows over-looking the straits. A series of small salons separates the sofa from the waterfront.

decaying selamlik, the men's quarters or salon, perched precariously on 300-year-old struts above the Bosphorus. The 'T'-shaped room, based on a form frequently employed in civil Ottoman design, particularly for master bedrooms, allows a fairly large space to be covered without recourse to supporting columns or massive beams. More importantly for the occupants, it provides a sitting area, projected over the water on timber supports, with windows on three sides giving uninterrupted views up, down, and across the Bosphorus to the neighbouring shore.

The salon was richly decorated with a unity of composition common among the best examples of Ottoman architecture from the sixteenth and seventeenth centuries. Travellers fortunate enough to be invited inside often marvelled at the yali's splendid ceiling. 'This ceiling, and the room to which it belongs,' wrote one American visitor, 'is the most precious thing of its kind in all Constantinople, if not in all the world.' Moresque stalactites in various colours rise above a Persian-style cornice painted in gold and azure blue.

The articulation of the ceiling relates directly to the plan of the room, with three rectangular panels framing an off-centre square. A circle inscribed within the square gives the sense of a flattened cupola, where a central pendulant of wooden stalactites probably supported a luxuriant chandelier. Much of the detailing incorporates Arab and Persian influences, which the Seljuks used so successfully in their mosques and theological schools in Konya and elsewhere. Floral decoration in an Ottomanized Persian style adorns the central section; while the three rectangles are decorated with geometric motifs originating from the Arabic world.

Above the low windows on the west side a subtly gilded and carved shelf runs around the walls, continuing on the landward side above the doors, built-in cupboards, and carved niches. Over this rises a frieze of painted panels, with vases of tulips, roses, marguerites, and lilies, each framed within a pointed arch. The faience jars, depicted in blue and white, were probably modelled on ceramics from Kütahya, the second most important ceramic centre during the Ottoman period. This painted decoration, probably the most remarkable aspect of the whole interior, reflects the composition and colouration used by Ottoman artists in buildings, ceramics, and fabrics during the sixteenth and seventeenth centuries.

The Köprülü yali was built for the fifth member of the influential Köprülü dynasty which provided strong and effective leadership during the last years of Ottoman expansion and the beginnings of decline. The first Köprülü, Mehmet Pasha, an Albanian conscripted through the devshirme system in which Christian boys were brought from the provinces to be brought up as Janissaries, rose slowly through the Ottoman bureaucracy working in the palace kitchen, the imperial treasury, and the market police. He then served as a vizier and governor of Trabzon before, aged nearly eighty, when most men would have been content with retirement, he was finally offered the post of Grand Vizier. In his new role Mehmet Pasha soon proved to be a ruthless tyrant, banishing and killing his opponents at will. One grand admiral, Topal Mehmet Pasha, was executed for failing to defeat a Venetian fleet.

Mehmet Köprülü built up more power than any other Grand Vizier for a century and a half, and more than deserved his popular title of Mehmet the Cruel. His cruelty, however, was balanced by the intellect of his son, Fazil Ahmet Pasha, who encouraged Mehmet to found an important library which still stands in the Sultanahmet area of the old city, an invaluable repository of seventeenth-century books and manuscripts. Nearby lies Mehmet's mosque and tomb, the latter

OPPOSITE In the oval-shaped upper sofa of the Sa'dullah Pasha yali a raised platform and recessed bay looks out over the Bosphorus and provides a fine setting for a collection of tombak or traditional copperware. Its domed ceiling is painted with rope-like beading derived from an otag, a form of Turkish tent. Naïve landscape paintings and a baroque wall fountain fill small niches; while the door pediments are decorated with intricate foliate designs, a theatrical touch influenced by baroque rhetoric.

ABOVE LEFT A decorative boss at the centre of the domed ceiling ties together the rope-like beading.

BELOW LEFT A series of eighteenth-century watercolours by an unknown Italian artist decorates a recessed sitting area in the Sa'dullah Pasha yali.

The garden entrance to the octagonal ground-floor sofa. The recessed bay is separated from the central area by two columns and low balustrades, a typical feature of traditional Ottoman yalis.

The upper sofa looks out over the garden and provides a traditional setting for Ottoman candlesticks, rare books, framed Imperial decrees, and a copper collection.

covered with an open grille so that 'the rain could cool him while he burned in the fires of hell'.

Fazil Ahmet Pasha served as Grand Vizier for five years before being succeeded by his foster-brother, Kara Mustafa Pasha, who was blamed for failing to capture Vienna in 1683. The Ottomans rarely forgave their commanders for military defeat and he was executed in Belgrade for his soldierly incompetence. The fourth Köprülü, Fazil Mustafa Pasha, fared little better. He attempted to restore an efficient administration in the Sublime Porte and appointed the ablest men to key positions. But his attempts to reform the economy were unsuccessful and after just two years as Grand Vizier he was killed fighting against the resurgent Austrians.

It was against this background of weakening Ottoman power in Europe that Amcazâde Hüseyin Pasha, owner of the Köprülü yali, was appointed Grand Vizier in 1699. A member of the Mevlevi dervish order, he was more in touch with ordinary people than his predecessors and emphasized the need for economic measures to ease the peasants' plight. He encouraged agriculture, reduced taxes on a range of goods from soap to tobacco, and initiated reform in the palace, retiring inefficient scribes and employing newly educated Ottomans in their place. Although Amcazâde Hüseyin became the most important reformer of the period, he was principally appointed as Grand Vizier in the hope that he would be able to negotiate the best possible terms at the Karlowitz Treaty, signed by Austria and Turkey in 1699. The accord marked a transition for the Ottoman Empire: as territories, including Hungary and Transylvania, were lost in the Balkans, it ceased to be an expanding power and gradually fell into the role of the 'sick man of Europe'.

The terms of the treaty were ratified at an assembly held in the Köprülü yali the following year. Among the guests were the Austrian envoy along with the Dutch and British ambassadors, acting in the role of intermediaries. According to a contemporary chronicler the foreign envoys were rowed up the Bosphorus in a procession of three galleys, pulled by 300 slaves. Three pavilions adorned the largest boat, followed by another full of musicians drowning out the noise of the oarsmen. In the grand tradition of court spectacles oriental dancers and singers, acrobats and Turkish wrestlers entertained the dignitaries before the serving of a huge feast followed by sherbet, coffee, and a pipe of Turkish tobacco.

After the Karlowitz Treaty reforms were clearly necessary to save the ailing empire and Köprülü Hüseyin Pasha set to improving the efficiency of the army and reviving the Ottoman navy which was converted from oar-powered to sail-powered boats. But the energetic vizier soon met opposition from reactionary elements among the ruling class and he retired, frustrated, shortly before his death in 1702. The yali continued to mirror Ottoman decline. In 1774, the fateful Küçük Kaynarca Treaty was also signed here. Under the teams of the agreement the independence of the Crimea was recognized but the Tsars managed to gain territory along the Black Sea coast, opening the gate to greater Russian involvement in the region.

A THEATRE OF THE BAROQUE

Other early yalis to have survived include the harem of the Sa'dullah Pasha yali at Çengelköy, currently being restored by Ayşegül Nadir, estranged wife of the Turco-Cypriot businessman Asil Nadir. Built for a Grand Vizier in the court of Mustafa III in the 1760s, more than half a century after the Köprülü Hüseyin Pasha yali, it marks a distinct move away from the pure Ottoman mansion with a somewhat fanciful decor placing it firmly within the period of the Turkish

From the outside the Şerifler yali at Emirgan, named after the Governors of Mecca, looks like a plain pink summer house with a traditional cumba or bay window. *Within is a sugary-sweet interior of rococo excess.*

The baroque Sandikli Oda or 'room of the closets', a splendidly ornate side-room. The 'closet' to the left of the hearth is actually the entrance to the room.

Largely rebuilt around 1782, the Şerifler yali is the most ornate of the surviving baroque-rococo yalis.

Corner detail of the elaborate polychrome ceiling.

Top Detail of ceiling.

Centre Detail of the scalloped hearth.

Bottom Frescos depicting pools and kiosks decorate the walls. They were common themes in miniature painting and during the eighteenth century often decorated ceilings and walls of imperial palaces and larger private homes.

baroque. In Turkey this contrived, rhetorical style was adopted between 1730 and
1808, a century after the greatest baroque buildings were built in Europe. But
unlike later stylistic imports, the overstated language of the baroque fused happily
with pure Ottoman forms. Nowhere is this more true than in the Sa'dullah Pasha
yali, where the organization of the building remains traditional while some of
the decorative elements are derived from the florid language of the baroque and
rococo.

From the outside, the Sa'dullah yali, painted a uniform brick-red, gives few
hints of its exuberant, almost theatrical interior; an interior which the current
tenant describes as having a very feminine feel. From the garden a pebble mosaic
path leads to the main entrance, flanked by projecting bays and shuttered windows. Like the Köprülü yali it has an irregular rusticity but within, Moresque
detailing, timber panels, and arabesques are clearly a thing of the past. On the
ground floor is a traditional sofa, octagonal, with recessed divans to east and west
separated from the central area by two columns and a balustrade. The theatre really
begins upstairs in the upper sofa, an oval-shaped hall with an exquisite domed
ceiling. The form of the room and its decoration of rope-like beading is believed
to derive from the *otaǧ*, or Turkish domed tent, a felt and timber construction built
by the wandering tribes of the past.

From the salon, four pairs of doors, decorated above with carved and painted
timber foliage, lead to four principal bedrooms with garden or sea views and four
ancillary rooms. The elaborate pediments were carved in Edirne, an important
centre for master carpenters, where the best quality turban stands were made. The
salon has the feeling of a stage set with several entrances for the actors, emerging,
perhaps, to play in a family charade. The twin doors to the north of the salon open
to reveal a small musicians' gallery where Turkish music, played on the flute-like
ney, the kanum and saz, once drifted into the principal room to the delight of the
harem ladies.

The theatre continues in the bedrooms where each has a painted niche decorated with stylized foliage. These, too, appear as miniature stage sets, with painted
curtains framing idealized scenes of Topkapi Palace and villages dotted along the
Bosphorus. The stage floor is a curvilinear shelf, while tiers of smaller shelves flank
the painted backdrop, casting a glance at the stage below as if they were royal
boxes. In reality, of course, they were designed to display small objects such as
lamps, vases, and candle-holders.

The scenic murals were discovered under layers of grimy paint during restoration work and are stylistically similar to other paintings surviving from the same
period, such as those on the Middle Gate of Topkapi Serai. The *trompe-l'œil* effects
and naïve landscapes present idealized views of the Bosphorus, its palaces and
waterfront yalis. Two of the yali's owners served in the Ottoman navy and perhaps
influenced a painting in the south-east 'rose room' depicting a traditional maritime procession of the sultan's fleet. The naval and landscape scenes, however, are
deserted. Following the Islamic custom, figures are absent, so that boats sail past in
a surreal-like dream, their oars pulled by an invisible crew. While not of great
artistic quality the murals are of considerable historical and archaeological value
and provide a dramatic setting for a fine collection of Turkish embroideries, antique silver and copperware, known as 'tombak', and rare calligraphic panels.

Although built in the 1760s the yali is named after a nineteenth-century owner,
Rami Sa'dullah Pasha, chief scribe of Murad V and Ottoman ambassador to Berlin.
A poet and translator, Sa'dullah was also a constitutionalist; a political stance
which was to put him at odds with the reigning sultan. Like the yali's previous

owners Sa'dullah Pasha fell from imperial favour and died in exile in Vienna in 1890 leaving behind a grief-stricken wife, Necibe. According to popular belief Necibe, filled with loneliness and longing, refused to accept his death. For the rest of her life she wandered through the oval salon each night, dressed in the pink tulle gown her husband had given her, awaiting his return.

Another exquisite rococo yali has survived at Emirgan, a picturesque village on the European shore named after a Persian prince Emirgûne, who surrendered Erivan to Murad IV without a fight. The small single-storey yali, lying adjacent to Emirgan mosque, possibly dates back to Emirgûne's time but much of it was rebuilt, and certainly remodelled, during the late eighteenth century. Owners included a noted scientist, a head clerk of the Imperial Treasury, and Aga Hüseyin Pasha. The latter was involved in the abolition of the troublesome Janissary corps and subsequently served as the first 'serasker', or commander, of the new army, 'The Trained Victorious Soldiers of Muhammad', founded in 1826. The yali, however, is named after a Sherif of Mecca, Abdullah Pasha.

Like the Sa'dullah Pasha yali, the Şerifler house hides its ornate interior behind an unassuming vernacular façade, although there was decorative woodwork around the windows (removed during recent restoration). Only the selamlik, an intimate interior of interconnected rooms, centred on an octagonal pool and fountain, survives. The plan remains traditional while the decor is a lively mix of rococo motifs with an astonishing ceiling framed in multi-coloured bands of red, yellow, and blue, and painted with scenes depicting rustic kiosks beside small pools. In a gilded side-room a rococo-crested hearth is clearly related to eighteenth-century interiors at Topkapi Serai, including the hearth in Selim III's room and the fountain in the royal salon.

In 1917 an American visitor, H. G. Dwight, noted the contrast of styles between the rococo decor and the modern European furniture: 'And it is quaint to see what an air, both whimsical and distinguished, that faded eighteenth-century decoration gains from the ugly modern furniture set about a fountain in the cross-shaped saloon of these descendants of the Prophet.' The recently restored decor is no longer faded, but French period furniture still contrasts with the traditional divans and a splendid marble fountain.

As Dwight noted, the main room has the common cruciform plan but side rooms have been pushed to the rear of the building, leaving the corner areas void and allowing more light to reach the sitting areas. Eighteenth-century yalis like the Şerifler and Sa'dullah Pasha houses varied greatly in size and ornateness but they were united by a common layout and projecting sitting-rooms. It was not until the nineteenth century that great changes occurred in the basic layout and the archetypical divan seating was abandoned in favour of free-standing furniture.

LOUIS XVI AND AN EGYPTIAN PRINCE

Most of the older yalis to have survived belong to a third period, the nineteenth-century era of 'empire' and cosmopolitan architecture where eclecticism seemed to be the only rule of the day. Earlier Ottoman tradition was rejected as angled doors leading off a central sofa disappeared, giving way to a more complex rectilinear plan. The solid window covers, so typical of the Köprülü and Sa'dullah yalis, were replaced by lighter grilles and shutters. Instead of corbelled windows and sitting areas projecting over the Bosphorus, sea-front doors often opened directly on to a narrow jetty.

Nineteenth-century yalis, such as those built for the daughters of Sultan Abdul

OVERLEAF *Sait Halim Pasha yali seen from the water.*

OPPOSITE Two stone lions brought from Egypt in 1860 guard the quay of the mid-nineteenth-century Sait Halim Pasha yali, also known as the 'yali of the pink lions'.

ABOVE Based on western neo-classicism, the façade of the Sait Halim Pasha yali illustrates the influence of European architecture during the period referred to as the 'Empire' style (1808–67), emulating the French use of the term.

A single window in the Sait Halim Pasha yali includes a central 'jalousie' screen which moved up and down in timber grooves. In the lower position it offered women within a considerable degree of privacy, allowing them to see the world go by without themselves being seen.

Mecit, tended to be concentrated along the European shore between Ortaköy and Tarabya. Emine Foat Tugay, in a book chronicling her girlhood along the Bosphorus at the beginning of the century, claimed that one of the largest, Princess Zeyneb's yali at Bebek, was designed by the architect of the Paris Opera House, Charles Garnier. The claim, however, is fanciful and probably derives from rumours spread by yali owners who sought to associate their Bosphorus homes with famous architects from abroad. No trace of the building remains today but Emine Foat Tugay described it as 'possibly one of the largest residences made entirely of timber ever known'. Old timber from ancient ships was used for the columns and beams, and parquet flooring was laid in the selamlik.

Less huge but still impressive and among the best kept of the empire-style mansions, the Sait Halim Pasha yali at Yeniköy, also known as 'the yali of the pink lions', stands as a memorial to late Ottoman taste. It was purchased by the father of Sait Halim Pasha from a Greek patrician, Nikolaos Aristarhos Logothetes of Fener, a traditional Greek area near the Golden Horn, during the 1860s. Sait Halim Pasha, an Egyptian prince and aristocrat, held a number of important posts in the Ottoman administration, becoming a provincial governor in 1888. Two years later he was appointed Governor General of the European Provinces, ending his career as Grand Vizier, a post he held during the tumultuous years of the First World War.

After taking up residence at Yeniköy in the early 1890s, Sait Halim Pasha made few significant changes to the main building but he added several annexes, extending the yali towards the road, and modified and refurbished the interior to suit his predilections and Egyptian background. Sited among waterfront gardens, the yali is typical of its time, with pedimented windows set within a façade of neo-classical proportions. Two arched bridges, one an enclosed wooden bridge leading from the southern corridor, the other, an open iron structure, from the yali garden, spanned the road and led into the park behind. Like many others that once allowed women to come and go without being seen from the street, they have now disappeared, demolished to make way for wider roads. The only bridge of this type still standing is the grand imperial bridge at Çirağan palace.

The layout of the interior, originally based on the plans of earlier yalis, was changed to reflect the nineteenth-century idiom. The traditional sofa, the heart of the Ottoman house, became a grand reception hall on the ground floor of the selamlik. Above, a second hall, of slightly more slender proportions, enjoyed direct access to the harem where smaller side-rooms – the gold, Japanese, and Venetian rooms – were the province of the ladies of the household. The original alcoves of the sofa were walled in, creating rooms facing the sea.

Fixtures and furnishings are unashamedly eclectic, a mélange of east and west where Louis XVI meets Egyptian aristocracy in an Ottoman setting. Many interiors, inspired by French design of the late eighteenth and nineteenth centuries, include panelled walls enriched by egg-and-dart and acanthus mouldings on the cornice. Corinthian columns support the main rooms and ceilings are decorated with central medallions and ornate gilded reliefs. An Egyptian flavour is most evident in the reception room and study. The former is surrounded by a magnificent stalactitic frieze, an Arabic pattern repeated in the deep pelmets dripping with gilt. Four double doors, lacquered and inlaid with ivory and mother-of-pearl, lead from this rich gold-brown room.

A pure Ottoman contribution to the building appears in the spacious porch leading into the men's quarters, where multiple panels of Kütahya tiles, forming floral sprays of tulip blooms and leaves, decorate the lower wall. By the end of the nineteenth century Turkish ceramics had passed their artistic peak, but these are reasonable examples of their time with designs in blue, green, yellow, and Iznik red. Floral themes continue above the tiles in a pair of windows flanking the entrance. Based on earlier Ottoman designs, sinuous ribs delineate a small pane shaped to resemble a tulip bud. Also in the entrance hall, several turban stands continue the Ottoman theme and hark back to earlier periods in Turkish history.

Furnishings are equally eclectic, although particular styles tend to be confined to specific rooms. French influence dominates with Louis XVI suites and corner cabinets, but there are also Japanese prints and a heavy Renaissance-style chest and mantelpiece, influenced by Italian design. Bronze figures, cast in Paris by D.Puch and others, of winged maidens, female nudes, and a young musician reinforce the Ottoman appreciation of, or fashion for, French design. On the walls oil paintings, landscapes and orientalist works, by minor European artists such as Narcisse Berchére, Léon Dupré, and Paul Leroy, hang in gilded wooden frames. Among the few non-French paintings are two works by Salvaro Valeri including a watercolour of a zeybek folkdance from western Anatolia. Valeri was appointed joint director, with his fellow-artist Warinia Zarzecki, of the Imperial Academy of Fine Arts which opened in 1883 to provide a formal academic training in western art. At first all the staff were Europeans employed to teach the history of and new trends in European sculpture, architecture, and painting.

In addition to the European furniture the yali houses Egyptian and Ottoman-style pieces. An intricately carved lattice-work screen in the pasha's suite is typically Arabic, with turned wooden grillework believed to have developed from Coptic woodwork. Widely adopted in Arab art during the Ayyubid period in the thirteenth century, it featured in panels of Koran lecterns, window grilles, and dividing screens. Several of the largest units are clearly architectonic. An Ottoman console cabinet in the reception room appears to be based, at least in part, on a mosque *mihrab*, or doorway, combined with shelves-cum-drawers in the form of traditional built-in shelves in early Ottoman interiors. The arched stalactite section, carved out of black ebony, reflects the vault of a stone niche, while the turned columns framing the cupboard door recall the stone or marble cylinders often found at the doorway or at the *mihrab* of classical Ottoman mosques. A second console cabinet has affinities to an enclosed street fountain.

As wealthy Ottomans abandoned the traditional built-in sitting areas in favour of European settees and chairs, a free-standing Ottoman settee, combining oriental style with the merits of portability, began to be produced. A heavy, angular example, inlaid with ivory and mother-of-pearl, was specially commissioned by Sait Halim Pasha and stands in the reception area with other oriental-style seats, each upholstered in silk fabric from the Hereke factory. Round and multi-sided occasional tables, inlaid with geometric and foliate motifs, reinforce the exoticism of the Ottoman-Arabic rooms.

If Sait Halim Pasha's yali reflects the architectural meeting of east and west, it also witnessed shifting Turco-European relations and the last decades of Ottoman rule. Sait Halim Pasha supported the liberal views of the Committee of Union and Progress (CUP), which opposed Abdul Hamid's absolutist reign and sought the restoration of parliament. His yali at Yeniköy was searched by sultan's agents for subversive documents and, exasperated by the harassment and surveillance of visitors to his home, the pasha left Istanbul for Egypt, later moving to Europe. Like many of his contemporaries he continued to support the reform movement from abroad and returned to Istanbul only after the success of the Young Turks' revolution in 1908. Five years later he was appointed Grand Vizier, although real power

The harem entrance porch and garden, Sait Halim Pasha yali. The yali was
purchased by an Egyptian prince and aristocrat, Sait Halim Pasha, from a Greek
patrician during the 1860s.

Sait Halim Pasha yali seen
through the colonnades of
the pool.

Stained glass panels add a touch of colour to the harem entrance porch of the
Sait Halim Pasha yali.

The 'Egyptian' reception room with its deep stalactitic frieze, inlaid doors, and heavy oriental furniture. The Ottoman console cabinet, dated 1873, includes small arched shelves reminiscent of built-in units commonly found in early yalis and town houses.

In the reception room stands an Egyptian lattice-work screen. The central 'bay window' opened so that coffee or tea could be served from behind. The screen includes a Kufic inscription: 'The most auspicious words are those that are sparing and meaningful.'

ABOVE Detail of a panel inlaid with tortoiseshell and mother-of-pearl.

RIGHT During the nineteenth century built-in couches were replaced by free-standing furniture such as this oriental-style settee. Its walnut frame is inlaid with mother-of-pearl and upholstered in Hereke silk fabric.

in the cabinet lay with other CUP luminaries – the calculating stategist Talat Pasha, Cemal Pasha, and the dynamic Enver Pasha, all of whom had emerged during the crisis of the First Balkan War.

It was Enver Pasha, a German sympathizer who had served two spells in Berlin as military attaché, who paved the way for an alliance with Germany in the First World War. On 2 August 1914, Sait Halim Pasha, Enver, and the foreign minister held secret negotiations with the German envoy Baron Wangenheim in the Yeniköy yali. Turkey was subsequently dragged into the war and Sait Halim Pasha, resenting the actions of his colleagues and having failed to counterbalance Enver's growing power, finally resigned in 1917. When the Allies occupied Istanbul after the Armistice they were on the look-out for scapegoats. Despite his opposition to Enver, Sait Halim Pasha was arrested by the British, held responsible for the actions of the former regime, and deported to Malta in 1920. His exile was a brief one. The following year he and his associates were released but Sait Halim Pasha would never set eyes on his Bosphorus yali again. From Malta he travelled to Rome where he was assassinated by an Armenian agent.

ART NOUVEAU ON THE BOSPHORUS

While the best of the earlier nineteenth-century yalis were often influenced by western neo-classicism, later to be dominated by a riotous eclecticism, another style imported from Europe became popular at the turn of the century and produced several spectacular new yalis. This was art nouveau, a style with little place in the history of Ottoman architecture, but which had affinities with the floral designs of Turkish ceramics as well as Japanese prints. Many of the houses built in the style, such as the Nazine Sultan Palace at Ortaköy, have been demolished. Of those to survive, the Egyptian consulate at Bebek is a somewhat surprising example of secessionist and art nouveau innovation.

The architect was possibly Raimondo D'Aronco who served as court architect under Abdul Hamid II between 1896 and 1908, and designed a large number of buildings which combined Viennese secessionist elements with the decorative character of the *stile floreale*, the Italian branch of art nouveau, to produce a flamboyant regional hybrid. The Vienna Secession had been formed in 1897 and produced a markedly different art nouveau from the florid organic forms associated with Paris and Belgium in the 1880s and 1890s. Austrian designers developed an abstract style of their own, with geometric forms composed of squares, circles, and triangles. The linear clarity of the secessionists, incorporated into some of Istanbul's fin-de-siècle buildings, subsequently developed into the geometric deco shapes of the 1920s.

D'Aronco influenced other Istanbul architects, Greeks, Armenians, and Muslim Turks, to experiment with the new style which often degenerated into the superficial application of decorative motifs. Between 1905 and 1914, when the style enjoyed its greatest success in the city, hundreds of buildings were constructed which owe something to the art nouveau spirit, often combining elements of the neo-baroque and traditional Turkish architecture. The style was adopted by Istanbul designers who, like their European contemporaries, consciously rejected the conventions of the past in an attempt to find new architectural avenues as Turkey entered the twentieth century. But the local art nouveau was only one of many competing styles. Under the CUP and the Young Turks nationalism emerged as the dominant ideology among competing interest groups. As a result, classical

TOP Ceiling painting of *Anadolu* castle on the Asian shore.
CENTRE *Wallpaper detail in the selamlik ceremonial hall.*
BOTTOM Panels of Kütahya tiles in the entrance to the selamlik. Kütahya was the second most important ceramic centre in Ottoman Turkey.

The ceremonial hall in the selamlik, dominated by a huge
oil painting, The Hunt (1865), by Félix Auguste Clément.
Set in the Egyptian desert, the painting includes Sait Halim
Pasha as the central figure, dressed in Arab robes.

An oriental corner cabinet, based on a stone or marble wall fountain, is flanked by French figurines cast in bronze.

An upper floor suite, furnished in Louis XVI style.

The grand staircase of the harem entrance hall with its 'empire'-style columns and decorative cornice, largely inspired by French design.

133

ABOVE *Recently restored for presidential use, this eclectic nineteenth-century yali was originally a French school. At the time French was the most influential foreign language in Istanbul. The élite Galata Saray school in Beyoğlu provided a French-based education for sons of leading Ottomans.*

BELOW *Built by the architect of Dolmabahçe Palace, Garabed Balian, for an Ottoman banker, Altunizâde Necib, this imposing yali has recently been restored. A French baron, a Monsieur Vandeuvre, lived in the house for more than forty years during the late nineteenth century.*

Ottoman revivalism, typified by Istanbul Central Post Office designed by Vedat Bey and completed in 1909, became the dominant 'national' style of architecture.

Along the Bosphorus, however, revivalism was overshadowed by art nouveau which approaches its most ornate in the heavily articulated Egyptian consulate. This, along with a second Egyptian villa at Çubuklu on the Asian shore, was commissioned by the last Egyptian Khedive, the charming and intelligent Abbas Hilmi II. After inheriting the Khedival title in 1892, aged just eighteen, Abbas Hilmi followed in his family footsteps, escaping the dusty heat of an Egyptian summer for the cooler shores of the Bosphorus. Sixty years earlier, in the 1830s, the founder of the Egyptian royal dynasty, Muhammad Ali, had started the fashion with the construction of an Italianate palace at Beykoz, one of the first villas made of stone and marble instead of the traditional wood.

When in Constantinople Abbas Hilmi was occasionally received at Yildiz by Abdul Hamid, one of his few detractors, before returning to his yali in the evening. The Khedive used the Bebek yali as a summer palace until, while on one of his frequent trips to Constantinople, he was deposed in 1914 when the British proclaimed Egypt a protectorate. The yali subsequently served as the Egyptian embassy until the capital moved to Ankara in 1922 when it was downgraded to a consulate, a role it fulfils today. The building's Bosphorus façade is a rather awkward composition of bay windows and secessionist-like balconies weighed down by a heavy mansard roof, reminiscent of nineteenth-century northern French architecture. A central block is defined by two turrets and crowned by a rising sun, a common art nouveau motif symbolizing the hopes of a new century; hopes which were soon to be obscured by gathering war clouds.

The seaward façade is fenced off by ornate railings running along the shore. Every fourth post is crowned by a lamp and each section embellished with scroll-like pedestals draped with stone foliage. Other sculptured motifs and vegetal forms decorate the window and door surrounds and iron entrance gates. The building was originally divided into a selamlik and harem, now the consulate and residence of the consul general, each having its own staircase with balustrades of wrought iron flowers. In the centre an interior court covered with a fine glass and iron roof recalls some of Victor Horta's work in Brussels in the 1890s.

While forced to part with his Bebek yali at the outbreak of the First World War, Abbas Hilmi retained a hillside villa set among acres of woodland at Çubuklu. The ex-Khedive also kept a new 70-ton motor yacht, the *Makook III*, with a huge galley, and sparkling copper and teak fittings. It had recently been built for cruising the Nile but instead sailed the Bosphorus straits and ferried Abbas Hilmi from the Asian to the European shore, or to Sirkeci station to catch the Orient Express bound for Vienna, where he now spent much of his time.

The Çubuklu house is not a yali, but it has one of the finest views of the Bosphorus from the top of its prominent tower. Deep eaves, parasol-like, protrude below the turrets and shade small windows and their rotund, decoish balconies. The summer retreat has fine iron entrance doors, crowned by a distinctive coat of arms and protected by a deep canopy supported on long slender struts, reminiscent of those at the Köprülü yali. Within, a circular hall, hung with art nouveau mirrors, leads to a second hall with a central fountain surrounded by a forest of columns. The hall is lit from above through a splendid stained glass skylight. Kaleidoscopic in effect, the use of stained glass on this scale was developed from the fashionable use of glass in art nouveau design, although it clearly has its

The Ethem Pertev yali at Kanlica, built during an era usually referred to as the 'cosmopolitan period' (1867–1908). While the yali overhangs the water in a traditional manner, the ornately carved balconies, brackets, and barge-boards are typical of the late nineteenth century.

ABOVE Nineteenth-century yali windows and decorated barge-boards.

BELOW Details of windows and screens of a waterfront yali.

An Italianate balcony, raised on columns, projects from a row of yalis at Yeniköy, the 'new village', on the upper European shore.

137

RIGHT AND OPPOSITE ABOVE
The 'cosmopolitan' period often
made reference to several styles
and diverse cultural influences as
found in the *Afif Pasha* yali at
Yeniköy. Here, deep eaves are
combined with screened
windows, a reference to earlier
jalousie screens, with calligraphic
inscriptions and a small
'oriental' window. Elaborate
towers and an onion dome add
to the mélange.

BELOW *A* row of late
nineteenth-century yalis at
Yeniköy reflects the eclecticism
of the times.

Decorative carved woodwork on
the façades of yalis typifies the
'cosmopolitan' period of the late
nineteenth century.

Timber struts, reminiscent of those at the 300-year-old Köprülü yali, support the
porch of the Khedival summer palace at Çubuklu.

Ottoman precedents in some of the grander yalis and sultanic kiosks at Topkapi Serai and elsewhere.

At Çubuklu, Abbas Hilmi enjoyed a life of leisure but retained an interest in Egyptian politics, encouraging the Ottoman army to move into Egypt and promising the sultan that his former subjects would rise in support. In the event, the sultan's troops received little effective help and British forces suppressed pro-Ottoman agitation. After the war Abbas Hilmi's presence in Constantinople and his desire to regain control in Egypt worried the new King Fuad. To the sovereign's relief the crash of 1929 brought the ex-Khedive to the verge of financial ruin. Abbas Hilmi, now in his late fifties, renounced his claims to rule Egypt and pledged his loyalty to the king. In return he received a pension of 30,000 Egyptian pounds a year.

The Çubuklu palace was subsequently abandoned and the ex-Khedive's yacht sold to the British ambassador. The house remained empty for forty-five years until acquired and restored by the Turkish Touring and Automobile Club in the 1980s. Its original interior remains remarkably intact. Portraits of Abbas Hilmi and his grandfather hang above the staircase; animal motifs, sculptures, and tiles are common features throughout the house. In the dining area overlooking the rose garden rams' heads watch in stony silence atop marble pilasters; bears, carved in timber panels, forage for wild berries among the door jambs; and in some of the original bathrooms, including that once used by the Khedive's wife, tiled panels include paintings of hens, chicks, and turkeys, surrounded by a border of humming-birds. Some of the principal suites retain their original fittings and have been furnished in the art nouveau style, recreating a distinct fin-de-siècle feel.

Another art nouveau villa, a neglected ambassadorial residence designed by Raimondo D'Aronco, has also survived at Tarabya. Built as a summer house for the Italian ambassador, it successfully assimilates elements of traditional Turkish konaks and wooden yalis. Corbelled upper floors resting on wooden brackets and deep projecting eaves supported by narrow timber struts are reminiscent of the Köprülü yali, built two centuries earlier. Unclassifiable and eclectic, the building has an uncanny affinity to the shingle houses of America built in the 1880s and 90s. Renaissance conventions are also incorporated into the balustrades of the balcony and first-floor terrace and in the dressed corner stone.

D'Aronco designed half-a-dozen other villas for Bosphorus sites. These, too, were based on a historical eclecticism, on a combination of traditional elements and the Austrian secessionists. Although most of his residential schemes were never realized, or have since been demolished, D'Aronco made a valuable contribution to the architectural debate as the days of the Ottoman empire drew to a close.

SPIRIT OF IMPERMANENCE

Of the earliest eighteenth-century yalis few still stand, although there are a considerable number of considerable architectural merit from the nineteenth century. The scenes that once enthralled Byron can now only be imagined from the drawings of European artists such as Thomas Allom, William Bartlett, and Selim III's architect, Anton Ignaz Melling, and from innumerable travelogues written to quench the thirst of a European public eager for information about the 'mysterious east'. Enough of the wooden splendours survive, however, many newly painted after recent repairs, to give some idea of how life was lived by the wealthy during the last years of Ottoman rule.

Eight pairs of double columns
surround a free-standing fountain
in the entrance hall of the
Egyptian summer house at
Çubuklu. Built by the Khedive's
architect, an Italian, Delfo
Seminati, the summer retreat
was based on an Italianate villa
combined with art nouveau
elements and Ottoman vernacular
tradition.

An art nouveau door leads into
the Egyptian summer house at
Çubuklu.

ABOVE RIGHT Ornate art
nouveau railings run along the
shore in front of the Egyptian
consulate at Bebek.

BELOW RIGHT The eclectic,
partially art nouveau, Egyptian
consulate at Bebek was
commissioned by the last
Egyptian Khedive, Abbas Hilmi
II, who spent his summers on
the Bosphorus shores. The
building combines a French-sty
mansard roof with decorative
elements derived from the
Viennese Secessionists, the
Austrian branch of art nouveau

Built in 1911 the *Koç yali*, owned by one of Turkey's leading industrialists, at *Anadolu Hisar on the* Asian *shore.*

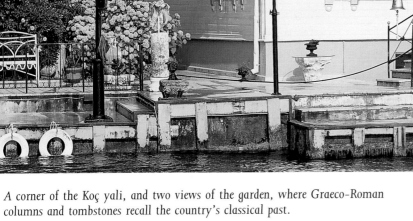

A corner of the Koç yali, and two views of the garden, where Graeco-Roman columns and tombstones recall the country's classical past.

ABOVE *The downstairs sofa with
its European and Turkish
furnishings.*

BELOW *Although only built in
1911, the Koç yali retains some
traditional features including a
slightly raised sitting area set
behind low balustrades, as seen
here in the upper sofa.*

While favoured pashas lived well, many fell on hard times, forcing them to
neglect their waterfront homes. Many visitors were struck by the general air of
decay. In 1911, Le Corbusier and his friend Auguste Klipstein travelled to Istanbul
where 'as the ship's wake was rapidly opening to touch the green banks of the
Bosphorus, our hearts filled with melancholy at the sight of the wooden konaks
disappearing into the water'.

The eccentric French novelist and staunch Turcophile Pierre Loti also regretted
the destruction of the old houses. In the preface to an illustrated album about the
seventeenth-century Köprülü Hüseyin Pasha yali, he noted recent changes along
the Bosphorus. Writing in 1915, he described the European shore as already ruined
by 'modern barbarity'. Only on the Asian shore was one able to find the lingering
enchantment, peace, and charm of the past.

For the Ottomans, buildings were often regarded as temporary structures to be
renewed with each generation, as the pocket or fancy dictated. The mentality was
such that every forty or fifty years the old would be replaced by the new; part,
perhaps, of the nomadic concept of impermanence linked to the spirit of Islam,
subordinating material existence to the afterlife. As Julia Pardoe noted more than
150 years ago: 'Turkey is a country where the population do not fall back on the
past, where they are almost careless of the future, and where the present is every-
thing.' Elements of decayed private homes, however, were occasionally recycled.
Some of the seventeenth-century tiles in Ahmet III's library at Topkapi are said to
have come from a Bosphorus yali.

Unlike Europe, Turkey had no formal aristocracy, with sons inheriting land,
property, and titles from their fathers. The fortunes of grand viziers and pashas
shifted according to the consideration accorded them by the imperial court. During the eighteenth century houses became the property of the sultan on the death
of the master, so that few were prepared to invest in houses that would outlive
them. Even if disgraced ministers continued to live in their stately dwellings, their
changing fortunes could be measured by the neglect of their homes. Even worse,
as Julia Pardoe noticed, were the abandoned homes of Turkish exiles:

> . . . the grass and weeds are rank in the fissures of the pavement; the hingeless
> shutters rattle in the wind; the mouldering roof no longer excludes the rain, which
> forms a thousand discoloured currents through the faded frescoes of the desolate
> and echoing apartments; doves build in the galleries, and locusts are loud among
> the garden-branches; theirs is the only song that awakens the deserted groves.

Only by a mixture of good fortune, compromise, and political cunning were
civil and military pashas able to live out their days in a manner to which they had
become accustomed. Yalis that remained in the same family for more than a
generation were few and far between, but if they did they were far more likely to
survive intact. This is the case with the Kibrisli yali, at Kandilli, named after a
Cyprus-born Grand Vizier to Sultan Mahmut II (1808–39), which has undergone
little change and retained its original harem and private gardens hidden behind a
high wall. Further down the same coast at Kuzguncuk, two sisters, Ruya Nebioğlu
and Ayse Bastimar, maintain the Mocan yali as originally conceived by a distant
relative, Fethi Ahmed Pasha, who not only built a successful career serving the
Ottoman empire but married a daughter of Mahmut II.

Even without the empire's social and political constraints the regular demolition of timber buildings is partially understandable. The problems of timber rotting in the moisture-laden straits would have been difficult to cope with without
the preservatives and renovation techniques of today. As frequently as they were

The dining-room of the Koç yali.

Calligraphic panels in the upstairs salon. Istanbul was an important centre for calligraphic art and a skilled calligrapher was well respected. Ottoman sultans patronized the art and placed great value on beautiful writing. Its practitioners designed ornamental book titles; decorative architectural elements, particularly for mosques; intricate tughras; and attractive panels with religious, philosophical, or literary sayings.

knocked down, the houses were ravaged by fire ignited by sparks from primitive braziers and wood stoves. And, to cap it all, as a taste for European culture developed during the nineteenth century, new buildings with Euro-frills were built in preference to the true Ottoman yali.

Efforts to restore early yalis date back to 1915 when the Societé des Amis de Stamboul began to raise funds for the restoration of the Köprülü yali, the remains of which still stand on the banks of the Bosphorus in a sad state of decay. The society, including such luminaries as His Imperial Highness Prince Abdul Mecit; the Grand Vizier, Sait Halim Pasha; the legal adviser to the Sublime Porte, Count Ostrorog; the Comtesse de Robilant; and Lady Lowther, the British Ambassadress, published an album of hand-coloured plates of the interior with a preface by Pierre Loti. Their aim was to conserve Turkey's important buildings and archaeological sites, but before work could begin on the Köprülü yali the First World War intervened. The Young Turks fought for a republican Turkey, and the sultans were pushed into the realms of history. In the new Turkey, aspects of the rich Ottoman past were soon rejected in favour of a western-style modernism and any attempts to restore timber yalis were easily forgotten.

The twentieth century has not been kind to Ottoman yalis. Significant numbers survived until the 1950s, but rapid urbanization, rising land prices, and fires – accidental or otherwise – took a heavy toll. During the 1980s legislation was strengthened to prevent demolition and inappropriate repairs, although fires continued to wreak havoc. Today, the few early yalis that remain, those illustrated in this book, probably have a more secure future than ever before. Existing owners appear committed to their upkeep, new money has ensured the survival of many nineteenth-century yalis, and in the 1980s the government restored the splendid Sherifler yali at Emirgan. At Anadolu Hisar moves are again under way to restore the Köprülü yali, the only yali to represent Ahmet III's light-hearted Tulip Period.

4

‡

BEAUX-ARTS ON THE BOSPHORUS

> *Outwardly it is impressive, from a distance, snow-*
> *white and gleaming, splendid; but within, in lavish*
> *lack of proportion, there is an astounding profusion of*
> *opulent crudity . . . In perhaps two centuries or less it*
> *may be regarded as a masterpiece.*
>
> J. A. Cudden on Dolmabahçe Palace
> in *The Owl's Watchsong*, 1960

During the mid-nineteenth century the shores of the Bosphorus witnessed a radical shift in architectural fashions. The classical Ottoman and Turkish baroque architecture of Topkapi Palace was rapidly abandoned in favour of a European-based classicism, expressed in the façades and detailing of several new palaces built by sultans Abdul Mecit and Abdul Aziz in the 1850s and 1860s. While Mehmet the Conqueror's Grand Seraglio at Topkapi Point hides behind mammoth walls, its slender chimneys and divan tower peeping above the treeline, Dolmabahçe Palace, a marble bulk of neo-classical proportions completed in 1856, makes its presence felt, set squarely on the water's edge of the European shore. The intimate scale of Topkapi's kiosks and pavilions was overshadowed by this grandiose monument based largely on European architectural conventions.

The almost wholesale rejection of Turkish tradition, represented by the sea-front façade of Dolmabahçe Palace, verged on cultural denial. In a city increasingly enticed by European culture, particularly French, the teachings of the Ecole des Beaux-Arts, the most influential architectural school in Europe from 1819 until the First World War, were eagerly adopted. To these new ideas other Latin-based elements were added and, in the façades of the Mabeyn apartments, Greek temple architecture was revived as a symbol of sultanic power.

The process which was to lead to the gradual abandonment of Topkapi Palace in favour of new European-styled palaces began with the reform-minded Sultan Mahmut II, in 1815. That year he moved to a timber serai at Dolmabahçe which was to remain the site of the ruler's official residence until Sultan Abdul Hamid II transferred his entourage to Yildiz at the end of the century.

As well as initiating the move upstream, Mahmut II started the imperial fashion for European dress. Turbans, seen as a reactionary symbol of the past, were banned, except for religious purposes, and replaced by the fez – the very headgear that Atatürk was to outlaw for much the same reasons a hundred years later. Mahmut was also the first ruler to drive around the streets of Istanbul in an open carriage; he attended operas, theatre, ballet, and receptions held in foreign embassies. European artists were invited to the court and often employed on

One of the ceremonial gateways of Beylerbey Palace, opening on to the quay and surmounted by a heraldic emblem of Sultan Abdul Aziz. The first Bosphorus bridge, opened in 1973, spans the straits in the background.

OVERLEAF The Bosphorus façade of Dolmabahçe Palace, completed in 1856 soon after the Crimean War. It was the first major Euro-palace to be built along the Bosphorus, although earlier palaces, now destroyed, had combined European and Turkish elements.

advantageous terms. Among them was the Italian musician, Giuseppe Donizetti, brother of Gaetano, who introduced Western music to the palace, and formed a chamber orchestra and military band.

The site of Mahmut's original wooden palace and now opulent stone and marble serai was occupied by a series of timber palaces and pavilions dating back to the seventeenth century. Dolmabahçe, literally the 'filled-in garden', had originally been a narrow inlet which was reclaimed from the sea when Ahmet I extended the neighbouring gardens by filling in a small harbour. According to Evliya Çelebi, Osman II continued with the scheme. 'All merchant ships at that time in the harbour of Constantinople,' he wrote, 'were obliged to load with stones, which were thrown into the sea before Dolmabahçe, so that a space of four hundred yards was filled . . .' The new gardens became a favourite area for picnicking and weddings; cafés were built along the shore and summer crowds entertained by jirit tournaments, in which skilful horsemen galloped after their opponents, their blunt sticks held high.

The history of the palaces which once occupied the site is poorly documented, but the first, costing 1246 purses of gold, seems to have been built around 1680 by Mehmet IV. Later sultans added their own palaces and pavilions, kiosks and fountains, and at least one villa which survived until the middle of the nineteenth century. The last timber palace, sketched by the German architect and artist Anton Ignaz Melling, was an elegant arrangement of interconnected pavilions, some with colonnaded walkways along the shore; others, the ladies' apartments, with latticed windows opening directly on to the sea. Three pavilions projecting over the waters were built, according to Melling, 'in accordance with the lethargy of the East, so that those within could fish for hours without stirring from the divans on which they reclined merely by opening a trapdoor in the floor.'

As architect to Selim III's eldest sister, Melling had a hand in designing the palace which, in effect, is a transitional structure between the accumulative Topkapi Palace and the monumental architecture that was to come. The timber serai had a flexible rusticity allowing, like the Grand Seraglio, for organic growth, yet it stood on the waterfront, open to the sea, unprotected by mammoth palace walls. It combined a Persian pavilion, built of stone and faced in tiles; a splendid porcelain pavilion; a central block supported on Ionic columns, introduced by Melling; a salon embellished with pearl and tortoiseshell inlay; and a marble hamam decorated with floral motifs. The rooms were generally small, furnished in European style, with chairs instead of divans, tables and mirrors, and tinkling chandeliers. By all accounts it was an appropriately regal building, but nothing could hold back the reforming zeal of the mid-nineteenth century. In the 1840s Sultan Abdul Mecit had the building torn down and the site cleared for his latest project: the new Dolmabahçe Palace, a monument of illusionistic grandeur.

THE BALIANS AND THE NEW ARCHITECTURE

The construction of Dolmabahçe Palace accelerated the process of westernization begun forty years earlier, but with its roots dating back to the Tulip Period. Under Abdul Mecit the rich Ottoman architectural heritage was increasingly ignored, something to be rejected rather than conserved. The young, open-minded, though feeble sultan believed that some traditional ways needed to be abandoned if his declining empire was to survive. Members of the Turkish élite adopted western fashions, some learnt European languages, particularly French, while entertainments took on a distinctly European veneer.

Part of the seafront façade of
Dolmabahçe Palace, a classical
temple front. Behind lies the
well of the principal staircase.

Bosphorus façade of
Dolmabahçe Palace, a neo-
classical/baroque mélange.

The entrance to the Mabeyn apartments, or selamlik, of Dolmabahçe Palace, where the sultan usually received his guests. A western neo-classical Renaissance design by Garabed Balian; the entrance portico is based on a Greek temple.

ABOVE RIGHT The waterfront entrance to the grand Ceremonial Hall or Throne Room. The façade is a complex arrangement of double columns and pilasters, with baroque ornamentation almost swamping the orders.

BELOW RIGHT Based on a Roman triumphal arch, a major source of Renaissance design, monumental gateways lead into the palace gardens.

OPPOSITE The palace's principal south-west gate, a lush baroque portal designed by Nigoğos Balian, Barabed's eldest son, who developed into the most accomplished and exuberant of the Balian architects.

ABOVE LEFT The selamlik gardens, central pool, and fountain from the entrance steps.

BELOW LEFT Lion sculptures have a long tradition in Anatolian culture dating back to the Hittites and ancient Greeks. The Ottomans, however, introduced statuary following increasing contact with Europe.

ABOVE RIGHT Dolmabahçe clock tower, inaugurated in 1895.

While retaining the veil, Ottoman women had greater freedom to travel about the city than they had ever known. Instead of waiting for itinerant tradesmen to call at their homes, upper-class ladies visited the city markets and bazaars in their carriages, buying directly from the shopkeepers and merchants. Those in search of European goods headed for the grand Rue de Pera, the central thoroughfare of the European quarter where foreign powers built their imposing embassies. Here were the most fashionable shops, including Stampa, which sold all manner of French and English items to homesick expatriates and the Ottoman upper classes.

As Abdul Mecit started to build new palaces he also adopted a more relaxed and visible lifestyle than his predecessors. While places for prayer had been included in the sultanic residences he continued to attend Friday prayers in the traditional Haghia Sophia mosque, in front of Topkapi Serai, riding through the streets at the head of an elaborate procession. He also began to travel outside Istanbul on inspection tours of the empire, wishing to see for himself how reforming laws were being put into practice. In 1846 he travelled to Rumeli and four years later sailed through the Dardanelles and along the Aegean coast to Crete, Samos, and Rhodes.

Back in the capital he was seen frequently in public attending the first Ottoman theatre, opened in Beyoğlu in 1840, and at ambassadorial receptions. During the Crimean War, when Britain and France were allied with the Turks against Russia, Lady Hornby described the sultan's appearance at a fancy-dress ball at the British ambassador's residence:

> . . . Adbul Medjid quietly walked up the ball-room with Lord and Lady Stratford, their daughters, and a gorgeous array of Pashas in the rear. He paused with evident delight and pleasure at the really beautiful scene before him, bowing on both sides and smiling as he went . . . He was dressed in a plain dark-blue frock-coat, the cuffs and collar crimson, and covered with brilliants. The hilt of his sword was entirely covered also with brilliants. Of course he wore the everlasting fez. There is something extremely interesting in his appearance. He looks languid and careworn, but, when spoken to, his fine dark eyes brighten up and he smiles the most frank and winning of smiles.

Winning smiles in public were accompanied by the establishment of liberal institutions and the beginnings of industrialization. The first railways, realized almost entirely by foreign investors, were laid during Abdul Mecit's reign. More than 450 kilometres were built in the Aegean region of Anatolia, in Romania, and in Bulgaria. Machinery and technicians were brought from Europe as factories were established to produce clothing and glass; and for the army, boots, rifles, and artillery. In Bursa, the first Ottoman capital, a Swiss industrialist re-established the silk industry which had gone bankrupt earlier in the century owing to British competition. Elsewhere, carpet-weaving factories, olive-oil plants, canneries, flour mills, workshops producing paper and cotton yarn were all established, invariably based on a model imported from abroad.

The new palaces of the Bosphorus rose in parallel to this rampant period of industrialization. Incorporating vaguely Italianate features, Dolmabahçe Palace confirmed the increasing awareness of and admiration for Europe. The palace was built by Garabed Balian, the best-known member in a long line of Armenian architects, nine of whom served under six sultans. The Balians became the most sought-after architects among the Ottoman élite and dominated the architectural profession for nearly a hundred years. While Sinan represented the pinnacle of classical Ottoman architecture in the sixteenth century, the Balians were largely responsible for the Europeanization of architecture three centuries later.

Like Sinan, the first Balian to be appointed as imperial architect, Bali Kalfa, came from the Kayseri region of central Anatolia and was conscripted through the devshirme system. The earlier Balian architects studied European architecture through prints and plans brought back by diplomats and government officials, but during the 1840s and 1850s Garabed Balian sent his sons to Europe where three of them, Nigoğos, Agop, and Sarkis, studied architecture at the same school in Paris. When they returned to Istanbul they brought back new ideas which, at first, were incorporated into their father's designs before they were able to branch out on their own.

Garabed Balian's largest commission at Dolmabahçe took the best part of a decade to complete. Heavy demands on the exchequer during the Crimean War hampered the final stages, delaying the official inauguration until the signing of a peace treaty in 1856. When the building was finally complete a magnificent banquet was held in the Ceremonial Hall to celebrate the achievement and the end of the war. Among the 130 guests were Lord Stratford de Redcliffe, the British Ambassador; Maréchal Pélissier, commander of the French forces in the Crimea, accompanied by the French Ambassador, M. Thouvenel; as well as the Sultan, his Grand Vizier, and the Minister of the Ottoman Fleet.

Dolmabahçe Palace defies easy classification, but it contains elements derived from the Italian Renaissance, the floridity of the baroque, and the classical-based teachings of the École des Beaux-Arts. Renaissance conventions appear in the southern portico and the colonnaded façade of the stairway hall, both of which are based on temple fronts. The throne room façade is a more complex arrangement of double columns and pilasters, where the decorative carving, applied no doubt for its novelty, almost swamps the orders.

Garabed Balian was the principal architect of the new palace, but his eldest son Nigoğos, returning from Paris in the mid-1840s, made a distinct contribution to the building, notably in designing the entrance portals and audience hall. The excessively ornate gateways which lead into the palace gardens to the north and west are based on a Roman triumphal arch, a major source of Renaissance design. Based on a tripartite division by Corinthian columns, they are carved with baroque-like twig motifs, acanthus leaves, rosaces, scroll-work, and eight-pointed stars; they have something of the lush invention of Charles Garnier's Paris Opera House built a decade later.

The lavish frieze is visually supported by fluted Corinthian columns, while on the northern gate smaller pilasters divide the walls which sweep gently round to two flanking guardhouses. Eclectic, yet within the boundaries of the European classical tradition, it is somewhat ironic that the Balians derived their classicism from Europe rather than the Graeco-Roman monuments of Asia Minor, so much closer to home.

Abdul Mecit's Euro-Turkish palace has a massive façade, 300 metres long, designed to make best use of the sea views. Divided into indistinct blocks, the planning of the palace enabled the Balians to explore the possibilities of a complex ground plan. Each block comprises a principal room – a reception area, salon or the main stairway hall; and in the corners of each are one or more ancillary rooms, mainly bedrooms and studies. This arrangement again recalls the cruciform plan of the Çinili Kiosk in Topkapi Serai, and earlier yalis, but adapted to a monumental European design.

In the centre, at the hub of the palace, lies one of the largest throne rooms in Europe. Designed by Nigoğos Balian, a talented decorator as well as an architect, the throne room is an awesome space of baroque excess. This is not Ottoman

OVERLEAF RIGHT *The grand ceremonial hall of Dolmabahçe Palace, one of the largest throne rooms in Europe. It is a room of baroque pomposity with huge piers and arches reaching to a towering dome.*

OVERLEAF LEFT *In the centre of the ceremonial hall hangs a five-tonne chandelier, a present from Queen Victoria to Sultan Abdul Mecit.*

A detail of the ceremonial hall's painted ceiling.

The painted dome, its trompe-l'œil windows wreathed in foliate sculpture and painted floral designs.

OPPOSITE The grand staircase, one of the chief delights of the palace. The stairwell is lit from above by an immense skylight. According to oral tradition the Balian palace staircases were designed by specialist architects.

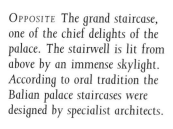

The grand staircase, showing its vast skylight and upper gallery.

baroque, a mélange of distinct character which dominated Turkish architecture for much of the eighteenth century, but a European import, designed soon after Nigoğos had completed his studies in Paris. Based on a cruciform plan, it is a heavily articulated room of piers and arches reaching to a towering dome supported by Corinthian columns in groups of four. The dome is wreathed with foliate sculpture and painting; and, within the circular composition, *trompe-l'œil* windows look out on to a blue sky and fair-weather clouds.

Visiting dignitaries and foreign heads of state were received in this theatrical hall and Queen Victoria, who was staunchly pro-Turkish, presented the sultan with an enormous chandelier which still hangs in the middle of the room. The throne chamber is flanked by the harem – a tradition that continued in the new palace – the sultan's quarters, and the apartments of the crown prince, now the State Painting and Sculpture Museum.

Second only to the throne room for sheer effect is the principal crystal staircase, a delightful atrium-like space lit from above by a large glass roof. The staircase displays clear baroque influence and is related to, though considerably larger than, staircases in the other nineteenth-century palaces. According to oral tradition the stairs were designed by a specialized firm of architects. Two flights, carpeted in imperial red, lead to a central landing; they then split, doubling back into two pairs of upper flights leading to a wrap-around landing. The banisters are supported by 248 crystal balusters (dutifully counted).

When it came to furnishing the palace a Turkish ambassador, Fethi Ahmet Pasha, recently returned from Paris, took an active interest in acquiring the most luxurious goods available. Shops and factories in Paris and eastern Europe received orders for Sèvres vases, Lyon silks, Baccarat crystal, and Bohemian chandeliers. Principal salons were graced with Louis XV tables and couches, Italian silverware, chairs from Maple's of London, and Parisian tableware ordered for official banquets. From the east, or existing royal residences, came Japanese screens and lacquered furniture, Indian vases, Persian carpets, and Chinese porcelain. A huge Turkish carpet covers the floor in the Mabeyn Salon, one of the principal reception rooms. Several silver clocks, decorated with jewels in the form of a star and crescent, came from the local naval dockyards. Today, these and other clocks in the palace have their hands set to five past nine, the exact time that Atatürk, the founder of modern Turkey, died here on 10 November 1938.

Presents from foreign monarchs and other dignitaries subsequently added to the luxurious display. Silver braziers and two huge white bearskins were presented by Tsar Nicholas II. Ismail Pasha, the Khedive of Egypt, offered Abdul Hamid II a fine silver cabinet containing a clock, thermometer, and barometer; and two large elephant tusks were sent from the governor of Hejaz when the province was still part of the Ottoman Empire. The decor would not have been complete without the latest in European-style oil paintings, dozens of which hang in the main rooms. Most, landscapes and city scenes, were painted by visiting or resident artists from Europe, including the Russian marine artist Ivan Konstantinovich Aiwazovsky, the French orientalist Victor-Pierre Huguet, Rudolf Theodor Rocholl, and Fausto Zonara. Other paintings, mainly battle scenes, are by Turkish artists, executed at a time when local painters were beginning to experiment with western approaches to art. Along the corridors hang portraits of the nineteenth-century sultans, Emperor Franz Joseph, Queen Victoria and Prince Albert, King Alexander of Serbia, and Crown Prince Ferdinand.

Of all the artists whose work was collected by successive sultans, the best-known is Fausto Zonaro, an Italian appointed official royal artist by Abdul

The first-floor landing of the grand staircase, delineated by Corinthian columns and banisters supported on 248 crystal balusters.

ABOVE AND RIGHT The imperial hamam, faced in alabaster imported from Egypt.

OVERLEAF LEFT AND RIGHT The reception room of the sultan's mother, one of the most richly ornate salons in the palace. Soon after the suite was completed, the poet and traveller Théophile Gautier noted the 'freshness and delicacy' of the painted ceiling, the 'arabesques with endless twists and coils, door lintels decorated in ornate relief, real or imaginary bouquets of flowers, the blue lilies of Iran, the roses of Shiraz...'

Hamid II, the last of the great sultans. Zonaro arrived in Istanbul virtually penniless in 1891 and his realistic paintings soon attracted the attention of the monarch. His skill was amply rewarded when he was given the grand title of Painter of His Imperial Majesty the Sultan and a house near Dolmabahçe Palace. Between 1896 and 1909 he painted around a thousand pictures faithfully recording the daily life of Istanbul and the palace. He also depicted historic events such as the 1897 Ottoman-Greek War and *The Entry of the Turks into Constantinople*. But he was a victim of history as well as its chronicler. After supporting the Young Turks' revolution in 1908, he was dismissed by the sultan and returned to his homeland where he settled in San Remo because the sea reminded him of Istanbul.

Despite the overwhelming Europeanness of Dolmabahçe Palace, it retained some traditional Ottoman characteristics. A distinction was still made between the public rooms, the selamlik, and the private harem. And each contains its own hamam. The imperial hamam is a rococo delight lit by a large skylight of glass panes framed in bronze. A delicate grey-red alabaster was specially imported from Egypt for the walls and fountains. The second, the harem hamam, with its less ornate fountains, has walls revetted in tiles of a European floral design, manufactured in Kütahya. In the centre of the cold room stands a unique round table composed of Kütahya ceramics with eight gold candlesticks on top.

The harem remained a separate though inseparable part of the palace. Harem women may have begun to admire themselves in Saint Gobain mirrors framed in Parisian bronze, but they remained confined to their own apartments. And instead of sleeping in western-style beds, a habit adopted by senior members of the household, they continued to roll out their mattresses in the evening and push them away during the day.

There also remained a rather curious concession to Ottoman tradition. As originally built, Dolmabahçe Palace contained no dining-room, at least not in the European sense of the word. A small room was set aside to entertain special guests, and banquets took place in the ceremonial hall, but there was no proper dining-room until the reign of Mehmet V in the early twentieth century. Instead, servants carried meals on metal trays and served members of the imperial household in their private rooms.

Nor is there a mosque, unlike Topkapi Serai where there were several. In order to attend Friday prayers residents at Dolmabahçe had a short journey south to the Dolmabahçe mosque, contemporaneous with the serai, or north to the older Sinan Pasha mosque, built by Sinan between 1555 and 1556. There was, however, a fanciful gilded room known as the Zülvecheyn, literally 'facing in both directions', where religious ceremonies were held, sermons preached, weddings and engagement ceremonies performed. During the holy month of Ramadan, *namaz*, or prayers, were offered here in the presence of the sultan.

If palace residents attended Dolmabahçe mosque they would have passed the new Imperial Theatre, opened in January 1859. Even more than the palace, the construction of a purpose-built theatre which, according to a French commentator, was 'somewhat smaller than the theatre in the Palace of Versailles but. . . even more ornate', confirmed Abdul Mecit's European tastes. The exterior was unremarkable, but within theatregoers marvelled at the silk fabrics and gold cloth hung on cerise-coloured walls, and the imperial 'poppy-red' ceiling. Largely inspired by French opera design, all the furniture, fabrics, and panelling came from France and it was M. Séchan, interior designer of the Paris Opera, who decorated the theatre to 'resemble the opera house in the Palace of Versailles'. Unfortunately

Detail of the crystal panelling above a porcelain fireplace in the Sufera, or 'ambassadors' salon' at Dolmabahçe Palace.

A round table of Kütahya tiles, a central feature of the harem hamam. The wall tiles were also manufactured in Kütahya but based on a European design.

The flamboyant ceremonial pavilion at Ilhamur, designed
as a fairy-tale hunting lodge by Nigoğos Balian. It bears
the hallmark of his earlier work on the Dolmabahçe
Palace entrance gates.

The ceremonial pavilion
is flanked by two raised
terraces supported on
carved stone columns, a
pattern that was later
repeated in the summer
palace at Küçüksu.

The staircase of the court pavilion, occasionally used by the women of the imperial harem when they accompanied the sultan to his country retreat.

nothing remains of the building where the Ottoman elite once watched Luigi Ricci's *Scaraccia*, *The Barber of Seville*, and *La Chasse de Diane*.

By the late 1850s Abdul Mecit's extensive building programme, the expenses of his wives, and the Crimean War had plunged the economy into debt. But the sultan remained blissfully unaware of the real state of the empire's finances. According to Melek Hanum, the wife of Kibrisli Mehmet Pasha, who served three short terms as Grand Vizier under Abdul Mecit, the sultan was surrounded by a 'court clique' of 'worthless and corrupt individuals'. A former chamberlain, Riza Pasha, and a son-in-law of the late Sultan Mahmut II, Mehmet Ali, hid the truth about the economic decline while they built up substantial fortunes of their own. Appealing to the sultan's taste for luxury, they encouraged him to enjoy life's pleasures, abandoning the reins of government to themselves. If the sultan ever showed concern, his ministers invariably got their own way by encouraging him to drink; it was one of life's pleasures which was often taken to excess by Abdul Mecit.

Sultanic riches were also squandered on the ladies of the imperial harem. 'The Sultan's love for his wives – and very numerous they were – was ruining the country,' wrote Melek Hanum. Nothing was refused them. They had as many slaves as anyone could possibly need; the palace was constantly refurnished; and, enjoying an increasing amount of freedom, the harem women drove around in the latest and most expensive carriages. The sultan ordered his wives to buy new dresses and spent an estimated forty million francs on the wedding of one of his daughters alone. Each passing year saw the economy plunge deeper into debt.

After Abdul Mecit's death in 1861 many hoped his successor, Abdul Aziz, would curb the spiralling costs of the imperial court, but he proved equally extravagant. The burly new sultan had no time for such sophisticated tastes as opera and plays, preferring cockfights and wrestling matches in the gardens of Dolmabahçe Palace. Under Abdul Aziz the theatre fell silent, although the palace remained the imperial residence and the focus of state protocol. When the sultans moved from Topkapi Serai the traditional open-air *bayram*, or feast day, ceremonies, held during the summer and winter in the courtyards of the old palace, came to an end. The gold throne was brought from Topkapi and placed in Dolmabahçe's ceremonial hall facing the sea. On state occasions, diplomats, guests, and the palace orchestra sat in the second-floor balconies; harem women looked down from latticed windows above; princes and deputies took their place behind the throne. Viziers, field marshals, ministers, and male members of the royal family were then received in order of rank with the most privileged rising to kiss the embroidered gold and silver fringe of the throne. The sultan remained seated throughout, standing only to receive the Sheikh-ul-Islam.

While royal ceremonies retained much of their 'oriental' flavour the extent to which Turkey was turning towards Europe struck the Honourable Mrs William Grey, the Princess of Wales's lady-in-waiting, during a visit to the Ottoman capital in 1869. Mrs Grey was impressed by the views of the Bosphorus and its shoreline palaces but disappointed by the city itself, noting that she did not feel herself to be in Europe 'yet there was none of that perfect Oriental look, with all the charm of imagination, which we admired so much in Egypt.' At Dolmabahçe the royal visitors were received by Abdul Aziz and dined at seven. The meal was well prepared and served 'a l'Européenne', but Mrs Grey found the evening a 'rather

A porcelain fireplace in the entrance hall of the ceremonial pavilion at Ilhamur.

Küçüksu Palace, built on a once beautiful meadow between two streams known as the 'Sweet Waters of Asia'. At the end of the nineteenth century the meadow was frequented by Ottoman society who were rowed up the Bosphorus in their slender caiques.

OPPOSITE ABOVE A view above the entrance porch of the waterside façade.

OPPOSITE BELOW Ornate double stairs sweep round a now silent fountain and lead to the main entrance. This is the view that would have greeted the sultan as he left the imperial caique and passed through the gate on the quayside.

The internal staircase of Küçüksu Palace follows the Balian norm of grand double staircases.

OPPOSITE The small daytime palace has just eight rooms on two floors.

Çirağan Palace, completed in 1874 just north of Dolmabahçe, was based on earlier Euro-Ottoman palaces, but here an exotic Arabian touch was added at the request of Abdul Aziz.

dull affair'. Apparently it was the first time the sultan had eaten in the company of women and no one spoke during the entire meal. It must have been a trying experience on both sides. Twenty-two dishes, alternating between French and Turkish fare, were served to the accompaniment of the sultan's band led by an Italian, Guatelli Pasha.

After dinner Mrs Grey accompanied the Princess and the wives of the British and Russian ambassadors to the apartments of the sultan's mother and wife. Compared to the Viceroy's harem in Cairo, the royal couple's previous port of call, riches were more in evidence. Every attendant – Mrs Grey found them hideous – was covered in jewels. Like the meal the meeting was a subdued affair. Following court etiquette, the sultan's wife, a Circassian girl called Mihri Hanum, was forbidden to speak; and, although a distinguished beauty, she was unpopular among the Turks because of her slim figure. It was fifteen years since foreigners had been allowed into the royal harem, yet Mrs Grey could only complain of the lack of a 'real Oriental look'.

FAIRY-TALE FLAMBOYANCE

While the construction of Dolmabahçe Palace was well under way Abdul Mecit, never one to neglect his leisure pursuits, instructed Nigoğos Balian to design a hunting lodge a mile inland from Dolmabahçe at Ilhamur, an idyllic woodland valley. The result is a delightful piece of fairy-tale architecture, a tour de force of flamboyant neo-baroque, condensing the surface language of the Dolmabahçe Palace portals into one small building. The lodge, with its horseshoe staircase and first-floor terraces, also became a model for the larger Küçüksu Palace to be built a few years later on the Asian shore of the Bosphorus.

There are, in fact, two pavilions at Ilhamur, the ceremonial house, the more elaborate and architecturally successful of the two, and the plainer court pavilion, occasionally used by women of the imperial harem. While today the ceremonial house is surrounded by busy highways and urban sprawl, as originally designed, the contrast between sophisticated splendour and arcadia remains the building's chief attraction. Like the Bosphorus palaces, it nestles against a forested backcloth, a true pavilion in a park. There is, of course, no Bosphorus flowing nearby, but water is introduced with an ornamental pond surrounded by marble lions.

Once Nigoğos's exquisite lodge was complete he moved on to build a second Dolmabahçe Palace-in-miniature on the Asian shore of the Bosphorus. Designed as a daytime palace, Nigoğos's next baroque offering is located on a once beautiful meadow adjacent to two streams which became known to Europeans as the 'Sweet Waters of Asia'. One of the streams, the 'little stream', gave the palace its name, Küçüksu, and it was here that the sultan relaxed on warm summer days after being rowed up the Bosphorus in his imperial caique.

Like Dolmabahçe Palace, the Küçüksu Serai was built on the site of earlier imperial buildings. Several yalis stood on this part of the seashore in the early eighteenth century, but Sultan Mahmut I had them torn down in the 1750s to be replaced by a wooden palace in the traditional Ottoman style. This, the original Küçüksu Palace, was painted by the French artist Auguste Préault and restored twice in forty years. It finally succumbed to Abdul Mecit's reforming zeal when it was replaced by the exuberant stone building which stands today.

The highly elaborate façade bears all the hallmarks of Nigoğos Balian's work at Ilhamur and the grand entrance portals at Dolmabahçe Serai. But even Nigoğos's flamboyance failed to satisfy Abdul Aziz. He complained that the building was too

In January 1910 a serious fire reduced the Çirağan Palace to a
smoke-blackened shell. It has only recently been restored and
opened as a five-star hotel.

plain, demanding more decorative relief around the windows and his monogram at the pediment. The principal Bosphorus façade, raised half a storey above ground level, is the most heavily ornamented, a sculptured symphony of oyster shells, garlands, rosettes, and carved niches.

When originally constructed for summer use no bedrooms were included in the palace, although it was later remodelled to accommodate visiting dignitaries. Eight rooms on two floors are linked to the central hall whose painted ceiling includes murals of Rumeli Hisar and Fenerbahçe. Whether intended or not the layout, with its four corner rooms and central hall, has its precedents in Ottoman design, most notably in the fifteenth-century Çinili Kiosk at Topkapi Serai. Ornate iron banisters decorate the grand double staircase which leads from the entrance hall to the first floor. In the days of the Ottomans, the sultan would have entered the palace directly from the quay, climbing up to the portico entrance, a fanciful dessert of stone icing, by a flight of horseshoe steps with its curling balustrades embracing an ornamental pool and silent stone fountain. Beyond the threshold the sultan would have been met with a view of the marvellous stairway as the doors were opened. Today the main entrance is on the landward side, so that the effect of entering a small summer palace is partially lost.

Following the Ottoman tradition of painted residences, the walls were originally coloured rose pink, with ornamental window and door surrounds picked out in white, like brilliant sugar icing. During the 1970s the palace was restored after structural weaknesses were found in the building. Flaking paint on the by now shabby façade was removed to reveal the light-coloured stone beneath. And that is how it stands today, although still cracked and leaning slightly towards the Bosphorus, with its stonework exposed to the wind and rain.

The Çirağan Palace grounds were entered by one of four ceremonial gates; two on the landward side and two opening directly on to the quay.

A TOUCH OF ARABIA

While Abdul Aziz continued to oversee Ottoman modernization from his base at Dolmabahçe Palace, where official receptions and council meetings were held, he began to spend more and more of his time at a third palace, Çirağan, just north of Dolmabahçe. Çirağan was another replacement palace for earlier wooden mansions where torchlit festivals were held during the Tulip Period, giving the site its name: 'decorative illumination'. Lady Mary Wortley Montagu described the old palace as being situated in 'one of the most delightful parts of the canal'. Some of the rooms were decorated with 'the most exquisite paintings of fruit and flowers', probably much like the interior of Ahmet III's Fruit Room at Topkapi Serai, and the central sofa included remarkable fountains where water fell 'from the very roof, from shell to shell of white marble, to the lower end of the room, where it falls into a large basin, surrounded with pipes that throw up the water as high as the room.'

The Tulip Period palace was demolished early in the last century and replaced by no fewer than three new palaces in little over sixty years. Commissioned in the 1850s by Abdul Mecit, the current palace soon became the sultan's favourite, although it was not finally completed until the reign of his successor, Abdul Aziz. Nigoğos Balian designed the palace along the European lines established at Dolmabahçe and Küçüksu, but here an exotic Arabian touch was added at Abdul Aziz's request. Artists were sent to north Africa and Spain to sketch important Arab-style buildings such as the Alhambra at Granada. Externally the Arabic influence is most evident above the windows where honeycombed stalactites decorate

OVERLEAF Beylerbey Palace on the Asian shore has been praised more than any of the other nineteenth-century palaces. Empress Eugénie of France was so taken by the windows in her guest bedroom that she had copies installed in the Tuileries Palace.

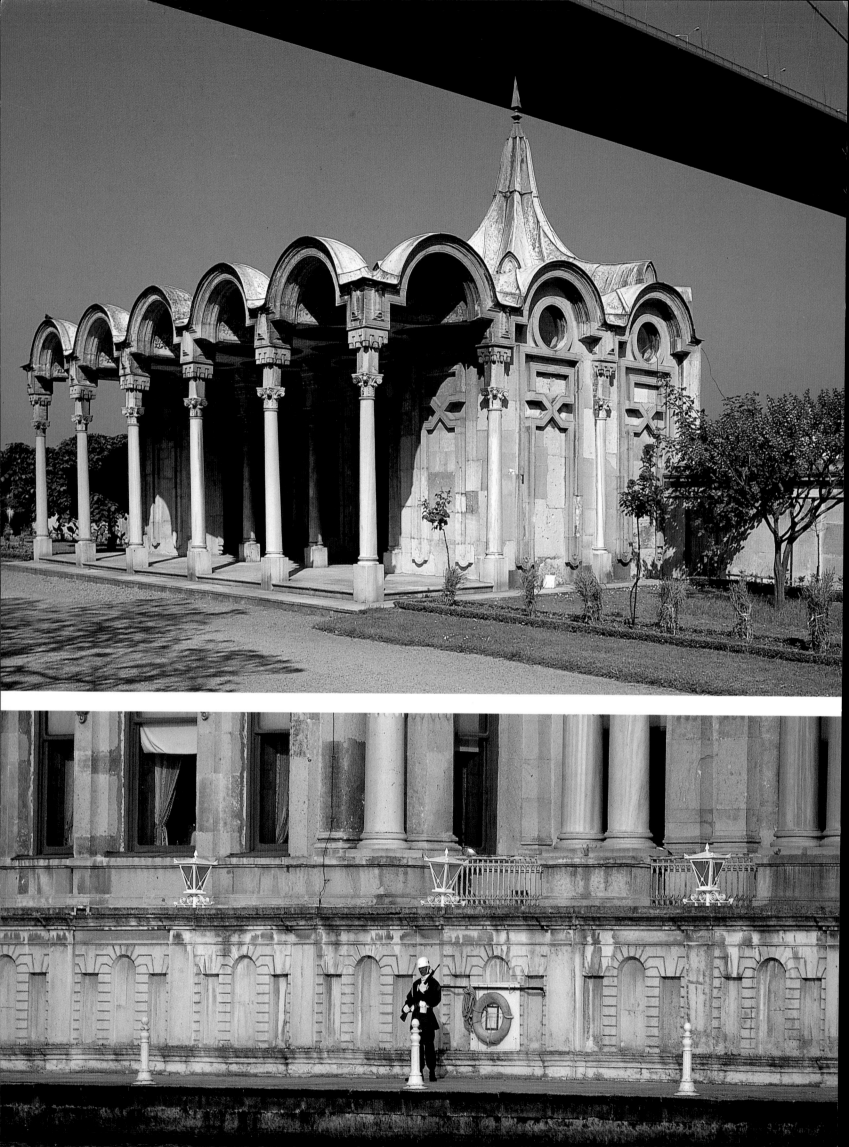

OPPOSITE ABOVE One of the two almost fantasist kiosks which look out over the Bosphorus.

OPPOSITE BELOW A soldier stands to attention on the quay.

LEFT Lions, sculpted in Paris in the 1860s by P. Rouillard, guard the main selamlik entrance of Beylerbey Palace.

BELOW Detail of the painted ceiling of the selamlik pavilion.

the slightly arched or oblong openings. Within, the Euro-Ottoman-Arabic mélange was more complete, particularly in the Ceremonial Hall and the Marble Pool Room. Contemporaneous paintings depict an exquisite interior painted in a rich mix of orange-browns, deep yellow, and blue-grey.

Arabic architectural conventions included horseshoe arches, sometimes with crenated edges or polychrome frames. One of the more impressive series of arches lined the corridor leading to the harem. Slim double piers recalled the columnation of the Alhambra; while niches and small built-in shelves were typically Ottoman. The ornate mother-of-pearl doors were so admired by Kaiser Wilhelm II that Abdul Hamid II presented one as a gift to the German ruler.

Constructed from massive blocks of ashlar, its colour varying according to its quarry of origin, the palace was given a uniform hue with a yellowish grey mortar mixed with goat hair. Anyone entering the palace passed through one of four ornamental gates, while a footbridge over Çirağan Caddesi connected the palace to Yildiz Park to the west, allowing ladies of the court to promenade in the woodland without being seen on a public boulevard. The bridge still stands solid, the last of many which once connected the Bosphorus palaces and mansions with their extensive grounds.

Abdul Aziz moved into the new palace soon after its completion in 1874, but only spent a few months in residence before deciding that it was too damp. He returned a few months before his death in 1876; this time he was disturbed to hear that bad luck would befall him since the construction of Çirağan had required the demolition of a Mevlevi dervish lodge, one of the largest in Istanbul. Fearing misfortune he returned promptly to Dolmabahçe.

During the reign of Sultan Abdul Hamid, the last effective Ottoman ruler, Çirağan was home to Abdul Hamid's brother Murad, who had been deposed after just three months as sultan on grounds of insanity. The unstable Murad nevertheless retained considerable support among intellectuals for his progressive and pro-constitutional views. At Çirağan, he and his mother continued to press for his restoration to the throne. Initially palace security was light and he openly received friends and supporters in his grand apartments. Among them was Ali Suavi, a former headmaster of the élite Galatasaray School in Pera, who headed a committee plotting Murad's reinstatement as sultan. Suavi enlisted Balkan refugees, grieved by weakening Ottoman power in the peninsula, to his cause and masterminded a plan to 'rescue' the former sultan.

On 20 May 1878, 500 Balkan Turks gathered in front of the Mecidiye mosque at Çirağan while Ali Suavi and a handful of his closest allies sailed from Kuzguncuk on the Asian shore towards the palace. At the imperial gates the conspirators struggled with the palace guards, seized their rifles and bayonets, and entered the royal refuge, meeting little resistance along the way. Led by palace servants, Ali Suavi and his associates hurried down the long corridors to Murad's apartments where they prostrated themselves at his feet, swearing allegiance to the man they hoped would replace his autocratic brother. They were jubilant: 'Long live Sultan Murad!' they yelled along the echoing hallways. But their jubilation was short-lived. Imperial troops had got wind of the incident, rushed to the palace, and confronted Ali Suavi, Murad, and their fellow conspirators as they hurried through the harem. In the ensuing fray Murad's supporters were routed; Ali Suavi and more than twenty of his men were mercilessly slain. Murad was subsequently held under house arrest in Abdul Hamid's new palace at Yildiz; and, according to one report, charges were brought against the palace surveyor for building such inadequate walls.

The principal selamlik staircase at Beylerbey Palace. Traditional Egyptian rush mats and a Hereke carpet cover the floor.

OVERLEAF *The magnificent Pool Room with its exquisite chandelier of Bohemian glass, dominated by a central fountain supported by four dolphins.*

Murad later returned to Çirağan where he lived out the rest of his rather miserable life. In November 1909, five years after his death, Çirağan was chosen for the newly convened parliament. But sessions were only held here for two months before a fire swept the palace, completely gutting its luxurious interior and destroying parliamentary archives. Popular opinion in Istanbul was convinced that terrorists, fuelled by nationalist aspirations, had started the fire. The official view blamed an electrical fault. Whatever the cause the palace remained an empty, smoke-blackened shell for more than seventy years; the sultan's marble hamam was the only part of the interior to survive. Several abortive attempts were made to restore the palace, but it was not until the early 1990s that Çirağan finally got a new lease of life. Its interior has now been rebuilt along traditional lines and the late Ottoman palace opened as a five-star hotel.

DOLPHINS IN THE POOL ROOM

When Abdul Aziz, driven out by dervish ghosts from Çirağan, returned to Dolmabahçe Palace work had been completed on a fourth imperial residence, mainly for use as a summer retreat, on the Anatolian shore at Beylerbey. According to Julia Pardoe, a writer with a superlative for every occasion, an earlier palace at the same spot was 'the most elegant edifice on the Bosphorus'. The state apartments were

> . . . gorgeous with gilding, and richly furnished with every luxury peculiar alike to the East and to the West. The Turkish divans of brocade and embroidered velvet are relieved by sofas and lounges of European fashion – bijouterie from Geneva – porcelain from Sèvres – marbles from Italy – gems from Pompei – Persian carpets – English hangings – and, in the principal saloons, six of the most magnificent, if not actually the six most magnificent, pier glasses in the world; a present to the Sultan from the Emperor of Russia, after the treaty of Unkiar Skelesi.

The new palace was as elegant as the old and impressed many distinguished visitors including the Emperor Franz Joseph of Austria, the Persian Shah Nasireddin, as well as King Edward VIII and Mrs Simpson, who visited it on 5 September 1936. A well proportioned building, less flamboyant than Küçüksu Serai, Beylerbey Palace is flanked by pinnacled marble pavilions, with steps leading from the quay to the water's edge. This was the work of Sarkis Balian, assisted by his brother Agop, and reflects their father's work across the water at Dolmabahçe. But the Balian brothers added a few touches of their own. The most evident stylistic development is the use of Venetian windows, perhaps introduced by Agop who returned from his studies in Paris, Venice, and Vienna soon after the premature death of his elder brother Nigoğos in 1858.

Within, the palace is typically Europeanized, a variation on the eclecticism of the French Empire style, with a few oriental elements introduced to the ceiling and Marble Pool Room. Among the larger salons is the delightful Blue Room, much lighter and airier than the sometimes gloomy interiors at Dolmabahçe Palace. Named after its artificial marble columns, the Blue Room was the venue for religious celebrations and is decorated with calligraphic verses on the ceiling. Even more appealing is the Pool Room with its marble fountain supported on the tails of two stylized dolphins. Abdul Aziz took a direct interest in planning the interior decor himself, instructing imperial artists to paint frescoes of calligraphy, Islamic patterns, and Ottoman battleships, a reflection of the sultan's fascination with seafaring. The maritime theme continues in the Admiral's Room, furnished with an extraordinary set of tables and chairs with legs and armrests carved to resemble knotted rope.

The main selamlik entrance is approached up short flights of curved steps and flanked by marble lions. Symbolically, lions have been placed to guard buildings and monuments since the beginnings of classical antiquity. In Turkey, the Hittites, Greeks, and Romans all incorporated the king of the jungle into their palaces, stadiums, and imperial gateways. Sculpture was not used in Ottoman architecture, although lions were common figureheads on imperial caiques, and it was only in the nineteenth century that animal sculptures were adopted from the fashionable gardens of Europe, particularly France, which, in turn, had developed the practice from classical tradition.

Sculptures also adorn the splendid Beylerbey gardens. In the lower garden bronze animals, cast in Paris in 1864, stand around an ornamental pool. A frisky horse with flowing mane trots among the flower beds; a supercilious bull stands its ground and kicks at its pedestal; a muscular lion plays with its seemingly petrified cub. Beautifully landscaped gardens rise in terraces behind the palace. Beyond, a wooded park, where deer roamed freely during the time of Abdul Aziz, extended into Bosphorus hillsides, but has now succumbed to highway engineering.

One of the most celebrated visitors to be received at the palace was the Empress Eugénie of France who stayed here on her way to the opening of the Suez Canal in 1869. Officials in charge of the imperial palaces, and particularly the kitchens, went to great lengths to honour her presence. European furnishings and cutlery were purchased, chefs were brought from France, and the senior palace butler sent to Paris to learn about French cuisine. During a 'week of festival and dreamlike displays' the Empress caused a stir among fashionable Ottoman ladies and unwittingly started a fashion for royal blue dresses.

As was to be expected, her tour of the city included a visit to the palace of the sultan's mother. But disaster struck when she arrived on the arm of the sultan. An outraged Sultane Valide stepped forward and slapped the Empress across the cheek. The situation later calmed down but Eugénie feared her coffee had been poisoned by Abdul Aziz's protective mother. Turks still relate stories that Eugénie and Abdul Aziz had fallen in love. One elderly Istanbul gentleman, who remembers the last days of Ottoman rule, eagerly recounts a tale that Abdul Aziz sent a sword to Napoleon III with the inscription: 'Il y a deux choses importantes pour un empereur: pèse et vainc.' ('There are two important things for an emperor: to weigh the balance and to win.') In Turkish 'pezevenk' is a general term of abuse, more specifically, 'pimp'. Had Napoleon's absence in Istanbul been noted?

Whether or not Eugénie was attracted by the bulky sultan, she was certainly taken by the windows in the palace guest-room. She had the frames measured and a duplicate made to fit the windows of her bedroom in the Tuileries Palace. On the same visit Eugénie was being taken to an official dinner being held in her honour at Dolmabahçe. Again the Empress became alarmed when the imperial caique nearly ran into another vessel. By her own account, it was only by waving her arms at the rowers to stop that she avoided a potentially disastrous collision.

Beylerbey Palace also appealed to Mrs Grey, who had been so critical of her visit to Dolmabahçe. 'I don't think I ever in my life saw anything more beautiful,' she wrote. '. . . there was nothing the least heavy or oppressive; and gorgeous and rich as it was, anybody might be happy to live there, which is not the impression produced by the other Palaces we have seen, and which, splendid as they are, give one no idea of comfort.'

ABOVE AND CENTRE The Blue Room at Beylerbey Palace, named after its artificial marble columns. Furnishings include Paşabahçe chandeliers, manufactured in Istanbul, carpets from Hereke and Tabriz, early Turkish porcelain, Austrian vases, and French clocks.

In the Mother-of-Pearl Room a French opaline vase stands on a Damascene cabinet.

Mrs Grey's praise would have pleased Abdul Aziz since he consciously competed with the excesses of his European contemporaries. His favoured pastimes included painting, Turkish music, wrestling, and cockfights and, like his predecessor, he developed a taste for foreign travel. In 1862 he visited Cairo and Alexandria, the first time a reigning sultan had set foot in Egypt since the country was conquered by Selim I more than three centuries earlier. Five years later he was invited to Paris by Napoleon III for the opening of the World Exhibition. From there he crossed the Channel to London to be received at Buckingham Palace and to sail on the Thames with the Prince of Wales, the future King Edward VII.

In part, Abdul Aziz's foreign travels had been a ploy to help silence his liberal critics at home by showing that he was far from averse to foreign ideas and influences. He had also hoped to secure substantial loans from Britain and France to prop up the flagging economy. But the sultan returned home empty-handed and his glimpse of foreign courts seemed to bolster rather than to tame his natural tendencies towards extravagance. He was the sultan of a proud empire and he had every intention of continuing to flaunt his wealth.

ROAD TO RUIN

Abdul Aziz now had four residences to maintain, as well as Topkapi Palace which he rarely visited, and the expenses of the Imperial Treasury rose substantially as new servants and staff were engaged to attend to the sultan's needs and those of his family. Burgeoning costs demanded a restructured administration to manage the imperial property and in 1866 Abdul Aziz created a new Sultan's Treasury at Çirağan Palace. This was controlled by a director of the sultan's personal affairs, 'The Marshal of the In Between', who became one of the most influential of Ottoman officials, equivalent in rank to a field marshal. The staff, according to one estimate, numbered 5500 and included scribes, chamberlains, servants, and courtiers, plus 1000 to 1500 women in the harem.

While the costs of keeping his entourage in style rose greatly he also spent freely on the army and navy, which he wished to modernize in face of the perceived Russian threat. During the 1870s the palace, much to the chagrin of the Porte's administrators, assumed increasing powers which had been lost by former sultans to Keçecizade Mehmet Fuat Pasha and Mehmet Emin Ali Pasha, two of the most able Grand Viziers and foreign ministers of the reformist Tanzimat period (1839–76). Ironically, it was the sultan's growing strength and inflexibility, combined with political changes abroad and a pending financial crisis, that was to lead before long to his grisly demise.

Although they were able leaders, the men behind the Tanzimat were poor economists. Tax collection was inefficient, foreign borrowing increased, and the budget deficit rose to crisis levels, leaving state employees unpaid and shopkeepers without trade. The sultan took measures to remedy the situation and internal dissent, both liberal and conservative, spread around the city like wildfire. As the era of reform began to wane, some underlined Sultan Abdul Aziz's role as Caliph of all Muslims; others talked of a parliament, constitutionalism, and Ottoman patriotism as a solution to the empire's problems. In the Balkans the Ottomans were losing provinces, and cries to save the empire reached fever pitch. Abdul Aziz responded by appointing a new grand vizier, the loyal Mehmet Rüştü Pasha, and by making the former incumbent, Hüseyin Avni, the new minister of war. The sultan dismissed any suggestions of a constitution, but his efforts to hold on to power were unsuccessful. On 30 May 1876, in a bloodless coup engineered by Hüseyin Avni, he was deposed and succeeded by his nephew Murad.

On that eventful morning Murad was residing in his apartments at Dolmabahçe when several ships and two battalions under the command of Süleyman Pasha, head of the Military Academy, surrounded the palace. At first, fearing for his life, Murad refused to leave, but he was finally persuaded by the Grand Vizier to accept the title to the throne. Abdul Aziz was initially sent to Dolmabahçe Palace only to be transferred a month later, on the orders of the nervous Murad, to a section of Çirağan where he could be watched closely. Just three days later he was found dead in a pool of blood, his veins slashed by a pair of scissors given to him by his mother to trim his beard.

Doctors called to the scene declared his death was suicide, but rumours soon spread that he had been assassinated. Some blamed Hüseyin Avni, arguing that he wished to pre-empt any possible moves to restore the former sultan to the throne. The accusations were enough to prompt Çerkes Hasan, brother of Abdul Aziz's second wife, to storm into a ministerial meeting where he killed Hüseyin Avni and the Foreign Minister, wounding several others in the attack. Hasan was promptly tried, convicted, and hanged, and the violent start to the summer was the talk of the town.

Soon after Abdul Aziz's death Captain Fred Burnaby, intrepid author of *On Horseback Through Asia Minor*, was at the beginning of his journey in Istanbul. One evening he went to a *café chantant* where

> a vocalist . . . began to sing about Sultan Abdul Aziz, of all his glory, and how at last pride turned his head. He did foolish things, went mad, and killed himself. 'But it was not his fault,' continued the singer, in another verse, 'it was his kismet . . . We are all under the influence of destiny. Sultans are like the rest of the world. Great Sultan, rest in peace!'
>
> 'But look,' added my companion, pointing to two men in the corner of the room, 'there are two of the secret police. If they were not here, we should very likely have had another verse or so, more explicit as to the sultan's fate . . .'

The mysterious circumstances of Abdul Aziz's death clearly unsettled the already unstable Murad. Although at first he appeared in favour of a constitutional monarchy and promised a liberal, enlightened regime, his health continued to deteriorate. At the end of August he was deposed on the grounds of insanity, returning to his apartments in Çirağan Palace from where he made several unsuccessful attempts to regain power. In the space of just three months a third sultan, Murad's brother Abdul Hamid II, ascended the throne. For the next thirty years he was to dominate Ottoman life during one of the longest reigns in the history of Ottoman rule.

5

✥

Pavilions in a Park

*It is not a Palace, it is a labyrinth. It has the air
of having been constructed with the unique object
of rendering pursuit along the corridors impossible.*

Yildiz Serai, Abdul Hamid's 'Palace of the Stars',
as described by an Ottoman minister

Yildiz Serai was distinctly different from the earlier nineteenth-century palaces built by Abdul Mecit and Abdul Aziz. Several pavilions were constructed in the vicinity before Abdul Hamid II ascended the throne in 1876 but most of the larger buildings were completed during his long reign.

In effect, the layout of Yildiz palace reverted to the concept developed at Topkapi, of 'pavilions in a park', surrounded by a huge palace wall, the complete antithesis of the relative openness of the palaces at Dolmabahçe, Çirağan, and Beylerbey. The sprawling complex became an expression of the sultan's mysterious and mistrustful character, which shunned the outside world. Instead of being a principal serai with a few ancillary structures, Yildiz is a veritable city within a city, a vast self-contained estate; apartments and pavilions including a guest-house and armoury, a theatre, library, and workshops, are laid out on the hillside above the Çirağan Palace among their own gardens, walkways, and ponds.

Abdul Hamid is best remembered as a ruthless autocrat, but at the beginning of his reign he proved himself responsive to fresh ideas. Initially he accepted a constitution and parliament which met, with interruptions, for almost a year. He made time to pray with ordinary people, to talk with Ottoman intellectuals, bureaucrats, and foreign diplomats about the problems of running an empire; an empire, moreover, that was in the throes of terminal decline. But before long disillusionment set in. Abdul Hamid began to distrust politicians and groups which, he believed, put their interests before those of the state and the dynasty. Foreign powers, particularly Britain and France, enraged him by emphasizing the plight of Balkan Christians massacred by Ottoman army units while ignoring the similar plight of Balkan Muslims. Abdul Hamid soon abandoned his flirtation with liberalism. 'I now understand,' he said, 'that it is only by force that one can move the people with whose protection God has entrusted me.'

The sultan moved to Yildiz Palace on a permanent basis after territorial losses during the Turco-Russian war of 1877–8. So inadequate was the accommodation that many of his entourage were forced, temporarily, to spend their nights in tents erected in the palace grounds. Abdul Hamid's apartments were more appropriate to his standing and there he remained, virtually cocooned, for more than thirty years, following his own concepts of imperial rule and fearful of attempts on his

Based on an Alpine chalet, the Şale Pavilion was the most luxurious of all the buildings at Yildiz Palace. The main section was constructed for the first visit of Kaiser Wilhelm II in 1889.

life. He left the safety of the palace compound only once a week to attend Friday
prayers; twice a year to attend religious ceremonies at Dolmabahçe Palace; and
once a year during the month of Ramadan to visit the Pavilion of the Holy Mantle
at Topkapi Palace. Even within the safety of Yildiz he lived a tortured existence. He
reputedly kept a loaded revolver to hand; slept in different bedrooms, which were
always well guarded; and was even known to change rooms several times on
sleepless nights.

Abdul Hamid built extensively at Yildiz, partly out of a desire for seclusion,
partly due to the inherited tradition that building, no matter what, was a sultanic
obligation. In order to enlarge his palace city he expropriated adjacent land and
property and demolished an entire street of houses. What he built was far from
beautiful. In thirty years he produced an architectural wilderness of mediocre
pavilions, curious kiosks, and timber chalets. The sultan even imported a prefabri-
cated summer house from Switzerland and had it erected near the harem in 1884.

Like Topkapi Serai, Yildiz grew haphazardly, but with little concern for architectural quality. The era of the Balian family, who had produced little of lasting
quality since Çirağan palace, was coming to an end. The brothers Sarkis and
Simon, who built many of the earlier Yildiz pavilions, had few of the aesthetic
sensibilities of their late brothers, Agop and Nigoğos, the last of the creative
architects in the Balian line. Sarkis, while the most dominant and influential of the
threesome, had always taken care of the administrative side of the business. Now,
with his youngest brother, Simon, he found himself responsible for taking a lead
in the design of Yildiz Serai as well.

Abdul Hamid later appointed an Italian, Raimondo D'Aronco, as court architect
and some of his varied designs were added to Sarkis's pavilions. D'Aronco's earlier
work in Italy, such as his 1884 project for the Victor Emanuel II monument in
Rome, had been dominated by the exuberance of the baroque. But towards the
close of the century he became one of the leaders of the *stile Liberty* or *floreale*, the
Italian branch of art nouveau, which in Turkey became mixed with the geometric
motifs of the Vienna secessionists and native elements.

D'Aronco designed many additions to the Yildiz complex although most were
never realized. Among his first projects after arriving in Istanbul was a National
Exhibition Centre which picked up but simplified the language of the Dolmabahçe
palace portals. The plan was abandoned after an earthquake in 1894. Other
D'Aronco schemes, however, received imperial approval. At Yildiz these include
the Palace Theatre, which makes references to the Paris Opera House as well as its
'oriental' context; an elaborate greenhouse cast in brass; and the *yaveran* or aides-
de-camp's building, now used by the Islamic Research Centre for History, Culture,
and Art (IRCICA).

D'Aronco's work was appropriately eclectic, well suited to Abdul Hamid's crea-
tion of Victorian boarding houses, Alpine chalets, Italianate villas, and rustic bel-
vederes. Ever mindful of Abdul Aziz's earlier fate, the sultan surrounded the palace
with a massive wall to protect it from attack. Abdul Hamid was afraid of his own
navy and confined their rotting warships to the Golden Horn dockyards. Yildiz
Palace was, he judged, a safe enough distance away from the Bosphorus shores
and the threat of a naval mutiny.

His suspicious nature led to continual changes in internal arrangements. New
doors were knocked through, old ones bricked in, rooms were divided, passageways narrowed, and windows walled up, in case conspirators should obtain a plan
of his labyrinth, smuggled out, perhaps, by one of his 1450 palace guards. Surely
they could not all be trusted?

The most important building at Yildiz was the Imperial Mabeyn, originally built by Sarkis Balian as a country retreat for Abdul Aziz. Under Abdul Hamid the building became the bureaucratic heart of the palace where the sultan conducted affairs of state and received the Grand Vizier and other senior officials. While the sultan remained the dominant figure in his complex bureaucracy, others shared the reins of power. Probably the greatest influence was Gazi Osman Pasha, hero of the siege of Plevna, where the Russian advance in the Balkans was stalled in 1877. The general's reaction to the west and his military reserve served to bolster Abdul Hamid's staunch conservatism. As Chief of the Palace Service and Chair of the Privy Council, Gazi Osman directed the sultan's personal staff and finances. In addition to representing the army he reinvigorated religious institutions, further justifying his title, gazi, 'one who fights for Islam'.

Lesser influences included the sultan's scribe, the scribe's assistant, and palace eunuchs. Two of the latter were held in such high esteem that they were given the rank of vizier, placing them above the field-marshal and scribes, and equal, in protocol terms, to the Khedive of Egypt, the Sheikh-ul-Islam, and the Grand Vizier. Able foreigners and members of minority groups rose to high office under Abdul Hamid. Among them was a Greek foreign minister, Alexander Karatodori Pasha, who represented the sultan at the Congress of Berlin; and an Armenian banker, Hagop Zarifi Pasha, adviser on economic and fiscal affairs. Another Armenian headed the palace Press Department, which translated foreign and domestic news stories and also foreign novels, particularly detective stories, for the sultan's pleasure.

Within the palace loyalty was maintained through fear. Spies and informants were placed among the thousands of servants, dependants, and bureaucrats to report on the actions and beliefs of the palace staff. The secret police, initially directed by one of Abdul Hamid's servants, also spied on the city police force, preventing the growth of any dissent there. Information received could determine a functionary's future. Those considered guilty of treasonous thoughts were dismissed, banished, or imprisoned. The well-known reformer and architect of the constitution Midhat Pasha served the sultan for three years while continuing to press for the restoration of parliament. But his democratic ideals were his downfall. In 1881 the sultan had him tried and convicted, on the flimsiest evidence and doubtful testimonies, of instigating the murder of Sultan Abdul Aziz. He was subsequently imprisoned in Yemen where he was assassinated three years later.

After his arrest Midhat Pasha was held in the Çadir Pavilion, now a café, in the palace's outer gardens, where others among the accused were tortured and interrogated. The trial itself took place in a marquee erected near the Malta Pavilion, where the deposed Murad V and his mother lived under armed guard. They had been sent here by Abdul Hamid after the notorious 'Çirağan Incident', the foiled attempt by Ali Suavi and his supporters to restore the former sultan to the throne.

While Abdul Hamid often feared his subjects he had greater affection for the animal kingdom. Part of the palace gardens was fenced off for a small zoo where thirty keepers looked after monkeys, giraffes, tigers, lions, and a pair of zebras. The sultan himself fed small mammals – moufflons, Highland goats, and gazelles – on walks through his personal menagerie. Birds were his special delight, although he allegedly strangled a parrot for imitating his voice. The royal aviaries were the most important section of the zoo and were added to with gifts from foreign rulers such as the Japanese emperor, who sent rare and exotic ducks. Parrots and pigeons were the sultan's favourites and an area of the park was designated a pigeon sanctuary. Pigeons, though, were still suspect friends. Breeding carrier

The neglected inner gardens and the fountain of Selim
III, built on the forested hillside 300 years before
Sultan Abdul Hamid II moved to Yildiz in 1877.

OPPOSITE The Malta Pavilion in the outer gardens of
Yildiz. The deposed Murad V and his mother were held
here after the notorious Çirağan Palace incident.

pigeons was forbidden in the city lest they carry messages encouraging plots against him.

Yildiz enjoyed more extensive grounds than any of the earlier palaces. Although designed by a Frenchman, Gustave Le Roi, they had the informality of English parkland, with fine old trees, gravelled pathways, innumerable flower beds, greenhouses, half-hidden grottoes, and free-standing fountains. In springtime the air was delicately scented by roses, jasmine, violets, honeysuckle, and, that essential Ottoman bloom, the turban-shaped tulip. In the centre of the park was a large lake complete with toy landing-stages, modelled on those along the Bosphorus which the sultan never visited. The palace employed 300 gardeners to maintain the grounds, with two Germans in charge of the Privy Garden and the Outer Park, and an Italian responsible for the winter gardens and greenhouses.

CHALET CHIC

The most luxurious of the buildings at Yildiz, the Şale Pavilion, was among the last to be built. The architects, Sarkis Balian and Raimondo D'Aronco, who had a hand in designing the Reception Hall, based the pavilion on a Swiss chalet, with deep timber eaves and decorative fretwork, a building of almost Alpine rusticity. Even though its fifty large rooms were sumptuously furnished, a mountain chalet was an improbable model for a sultan's palace. This rather parochial building form was a clear rejection of the sophisticated monumentality of Dolmabahçe and had its precedents in the 'stone tents' at Topkapi.

Although the architecture of Dolmabahçe Palace was largely forgotten, the former serai supplied much of the European furniture for what became the new state guest-house. Abdul Hamid also brought part of the vast collection of Chinese porcelain from Topkapi and decorated the new halls and salons in European style, with a somewhat lighter touch than was typical in the earlier nineteenth-century palaces. In the principal reception room of the Şale Pavilion one of the largest carpets ever produced, a seven-tonne Hereke measuring more than 400 square metres, was laid from wall to wall. It was so large that nineteen pairs of water buffalo pulling a timber cart were required to carry it the fifty miles from Hereke to Istanbul. When it arrived in the palace a wall had to be demolished so that the carpet could be installed. The sultan ordered a second carpet of similar size from Hereke as a gift to Kaiser Wilhelm II, but that had to be cut in two so that it could be loaded on the train to Germany.

The principal part of the pavilion was built for the Kaiser's first visit to Istanbul in 1889. Accompanied by his wife Empress Augusta Victoria, the German emperor sailed up the Bosphorus in his imperial yacht, the three-masted *Hohenzollern*, and docked at Dolmabahçe. Crowds in small rowing-boats and slender caiques surrounded the German vessel and welcomed the Kaiser as he appeared on deck dressed in his cavalry uniform and plumed helmet. From Dolmabahçe the royal couple drove through the streets in an open carriage, led by horsemen in turquoise uniforms edged in gold braid.

The visit heralded increased Turco-German relations and growing German influence in the Ottoman Empire. The previous year an agreement with the Deutsche Bank for the construction of a new railway line, extending the Haydarpasa–Izmit route to Ankara and Baghdad, had challenged the predominance of French and British interests in the Ottoman economy. During the 1880s Germany became the dominant supplier of agricultural machinery, it began to win lucrative contracts

An unusual fountain in the corner of the winter garden designed by the Italian architect Raimondo D'Aronco. The garden was probably reserved for the sultan's use and was linked to the imperial apartments via private passages.

The Italianate armoury at Yildiz Palace, originally built as a dining-hall.
Restored in 1984, it is now used for exhibitions, antique fairs, and auctions.

for military equipment, and subsequently offered technical aid to help build the Hicaz Railway, connecting Syria with the holy cities of Islam.

To commemorate closer economic and political ties, the Kaiser presented Abdul Hamid with a marble street fountain which still stands in the Sultanahmet district of old 'Stamboul, within the shadow of the Blue Mosque. German autocracy appealed to the sultan's attitudes to personal rule and he valued the Kaiser's friendship, although Ottoman intellectuals probably felt closer to Britain and France. By the time of the emperor's second visit nine years later, a new section of Şale Pavilion, the Ceremonial Apartments, had been inaugurated in his honour.

The new rooms of the palace were filled with French furniture, huge porcelain vases, paintings by the Italian court artist Fausto Zonaro, glittering chandeliers, a bust of the German Kaiser, and the products of the imperial factories: silk hangings, carpets, and sixteen porcelain stoves. The sumptuousness of the decor and the kiosk's heavy gilt mouldings were reflected in large mirrors, of which the sultan was particularly fond.

While most of the interiors were clearly Europeanized, Yildiz Palace followed the traditional Islamic pattern of a division between the selamlik and harem, and there were a number of distinctly oriental rooms. Among them, the dining-hall has a strong eastern feel with elaborate wooden doors inlaid with mother-of-pearl in geometric and floral patterns. Similar doors lead from the Arabian room in the Sait Halim Pasha yali at Yeniköy.

In the dining-room strict etiquette governed a royal feast. Ministers and generals lined up and bowed before the sultan took his seat. Until the sovereign raised his knife and fork, the guests' food remained untouched, and there was silence unless someone was summoned to speak. In an effort to please foreign dignitaries European cuisine was served as well as Turkish dishes although, judging from the accounts of one French ambassador, Paul Cambon, and Lady Layard, the Turkish food was probably better prepared.

Foreign guests were frequently invited to the delightful Yildiz Theatre adjacent to the harem buildings. Its pale yellow and light blue decor, highlighted with gilt moulding, made it a much lighter interior than the red satin luxury of the first court theatre, now demolished, at Dolmabahçe. The ceiling almost sparkles with more than 400 stars on a blue background. Touring troupes were invited to the palace to perform popular plays, *Othello* or *The Merchant of Venice*, or operas such as *The Barber of Seville*, *La Belle Hélène*, and the sultan's favourite, *Rigoletto*. Abdul Hamid sat in his private box above the entrance hall with ladies of the harem seated on each side, shielded by lattice screens.

'Since no one is allowed to sit with their backs to the sultan,' observed an Italian actor, Ernesto Rossi, who arrived in Istanbul with his company in 1889, 'the stalls are kept empty. Pashas, officers, and palace officials are obliged to sit together on the balcony.' Another Italian, Arturo Stravolo, made the sultan laugh so much that he was asked to establish a palace theatre company. He readily agreed and moved his family to Istanbul; but he had trouble finding sufficient women prepared to act on stage and men often played the female roles. Visiting companies invariably played to extremely small audiences at Yildiz and they rarely showed their appreciation. The sultan himself would never applaud.

Unlike much of the palace compound the theatre was lit by electric light. Elsewhere in the city electricity was forbidden, although allowed in Smyrna and Salonica, since the word dynamo reminded Abdul Hamid of dynamite. Despite Abdul Hamid's fears he occasionally ventured outside his 'city' walls, attending the biannual religious ceremonies still held at Dolmabahçe Palace. On one of these occasions, a trainee secretary, attending for the first time, was clearly surprised by some of the things he saw. Abdul Hamid's 'head seemed to have sunk between his shoulders', he wrote, but he walked firmly. A fanfare sounded as the sultan entered, followed by gentlemen-in-waiting, the Chief Black Eunuch wearing a fine gold and silver embroidered uniform, followed by the Head Secretary and the Court Chamberlain. The young secretary was astonished: 'I couldn't help feeling uneasy at the sight of this African negro standing at the head of twenty-five educated men' (sic).

At the end of the ceremony, after the sultan had received the civil servants, the military, and the latest graduates from the Imperial School, it was finally the turn of the palace servants. 'What a mob! What a motley crew!' raged the new secretary. Grooms and drivers, shepherds in thick jackets, poultry-house keepers, oarsmen from the Sultan's caiques, musicians, actors, and watchmen all lined up in the imperial presence. 'I looked on in amazement . . . what a commonplace thing a medal had become under Abdul Hamid. The driver whose hands had grown hard holding the reins of his horses and the groom whose clothes still smelled of dung both wore medals of the Ottoman Empire on their chests.'

General panic ensued at a later ceremony, held in 1901, when the palace was rocked by an earthquake. The central section of the four-and-a-half ton chandelier presented by Queen Victoria fell crashing to the floor. Windows shattered and a fearful minority fled the shaken building. It was only a minor tremor, no one was seriously injured, and when the ceremony resumed the sultan ordered a blacklist to be compiled of all those who had deserted him in the moment of danger.

A PICTURE TELLS A THOUSAND WORDS

Abdul Hamid was captivated by photography as well as by the theatre, appointing official photographers to document events and places throughout the empire. He preferred photographs to written reports since black and white images, he believed, were able to reveal political and emotional leanings far more accurately than a thousand words. Before receiving people he would ask for their portrait. He looked through family albums to determine which young men should be admitted to military school; and he decided which prisoners should be granted amnesty on the basis of a prison snapshot. In the palace library he built up a vast collection of 800 albums, which survive today thanks to a quick-witted librarian who prevented looters entering the library after the sultan's deposition in 1909.

Other western-derived art forms were also promoted under Abdul Hamid. The first generation of Turkish painters schooled in occidental techniques had trained in Paris during the 1860s, and it was their subsequent return to Istanbul which provided the impetus for the foundation of the Imperial Academy of Fine Arts in 1883. The academy was initially staffed by Europeans such as Salvaro Valeri and Fausto Zonaro, who painted a copy of Gentile Bellini's fifteenth-century portrait of Mehmet the Conqueror for the Yildiz galleries; but they were gradually replaced in favour of Turkish teachers. Among them the school's second director, Osman Hamdi, a Paris-trained artist, archaeologist, and distinguished intellectual, further strengthened its departments of architecture, sculpture, and painting.

In addition to the Imperial Academy and his extensive photographic library Abdul Hamid established an Imperial Porcelain Factory at Yildiz in 1894 to supply the royal household and the Ottoman upper classes with decorative ceramics. In the early stages of production a foreman and several skilled workers were brought over from Limoges and clay imported from France. A naval artist, Halid Naci, went to Sèvres to learn the craft of porcelain decoration in one of the foremost centres in Europe. On his return he accepted the post of chief artist in the royal workshops.

Designed by Raimondo D'Aronco, the Imperial Factory is an unusual building for the Ottoman capital. The low red-brick workshop is dominated by corner turrets with portcullis windows, reminiscent of medieval towers. Surface decoration, projecting brick detailing and marble banding, reinforce the analogy which was clearly appropriate for the walled palace city. Behind its turreted exterior craftsmen produced a whole range of porcelain items, partially filling a demand for goods that had hitherto been supplied from Europe. There were sugar bowls by Hoca Ali Riza, with idealized depictions of the Bosphorus; vases with paintings of the Süleymaniye complex; plates signed by Fausto Zonaro; and floral-patterned jugs. Like many of the buildings associated with Yildiz it was abandoned when Abdul Hamid fell from power. Today, the factory is back in use although its vases and plates are of poorer quality than those produced in the early years.

There was also an imperial carpentry workshop where Abdul Hamid had his own room set aside to pursue his favourite hobby. Some of the furniture in the Bosphorus palaces is said to be his work. In the harem dining-room at Beylerbey Palace, for instance, are a dining-table and set of chairs, inlaid with mother-of-pearl, bearing the sultan's signature in Kufic script. During the 1890s the royal carpenters at Yildiz began to produce 'Turkish Louis XVI' furniture, an adaptation of the original French style, somewhat stiffer and with lower seats than the real thing. In furniture design, as in other arts, Europe continued to exert a strong influence on imperial Ottoman taste, but Abdul Hamid also made great efforts to reinforce his role as a pious Islamic monarch.

GOD'S SHADOW ON EARTH

The relative ease with which Abdul Hamid had accepted the new art of photography was somewhat paradoxical, given the traditional Islamic taboo on the representation of the human form. While the sultan appreciated European art and some foreign inventions, he also projected and strengthened his role as the Caliph, the leader of Muslims everywhere. At the beginning of his reign he attended Friday prayers at Dolmabahçe but in 1886 had the hideous Hamidiye Mosque built just outside the palace walls. By mid-morning on Fridays, crowds were already gathering in anticipation of the selamlik, the sultan's public procession to the mosque, which, according to religious convention, could only take place after noon as the sun began to decline. Swarthy peasants, Arabs in flowing robes, and veiled women from the four corners of the empire, from Arabia to Albania, from Bulgaria to Baghdad, waited for a glimpse of 'God's Shadow on Earth'. A trumpet sounded as the Caliph appeared seated in a victoria carriage drawn by impeccably groomed horses. The crowd cheered in unison: 'Long Live Our Emperor! Long Live Our Emperor!'

Not all observers were impressed by the Friday display. Sir Charles Eliot had mixed feelings about a selamlik he attended in 1898. 'As a military display the spectacle is remarkable,' he wrote, 'as a pageant, disappointing. Turkish ceremonies lack order and grandeur.' The sense of anticipation among the crowd was heightened by the sultan who invariably arrived late, a tactic designed to foil any potential assassins while secret police mingled with the crowd. As events were to prove, his precaution was well-founded. In 1905 a group of Armenian conspirators in an operation codenamed 'dragon', attempted to kill the sultan as he

returned to Yildiz after the selamlik ceremony. Much to the relief of the attendant masses he escaped unscathed.

Under Abdul Hamid the palace became an important centre of Islam as a return to traditional values, undermined during the reformist Tanzimat period, was actively encouraged by the sultan. The influence of the ulema, the leading religious functionaries, was reinstated and prayer meetings held in the Çit Kasir, next to the Büyük Mabeyn, during Ramadan. On the sixteenth day of Shaban (the eighth month of the Muslim year), the holy Sürre-i Hamuyan procession departed from the Yildiz gates each year, loaded with gifts and ceremonial keys, for the long journey to Mecca and Medina. At the beginning of the century an American traveller, H. G. Dwight, watched the passing of a sacred caravan and was struck by a huge camel which 'wore a green silk saddle-cloth embroidered in white, and above that a tall green howdah with gold embroidery; and ostrich plumes nodded from him in tufts, and at his knees he wore caps of coloured beads.'

Reactionary members of the ulema, critical of European ways, increasingly promoted Islamic concepts of culture and civilization as a counterweight to Western imperialism. Abdul Hamid used the movement, led by Field-Marshal Gazi Osman Pasha, to strengthen his position at home and among other Muslims beyond the contracting borders of the empire. Muslim schools flourished, funded by the state treasury, and Arabic and Islamic studies were included in the curricula of secular schools. The celebration of religious holidays was encouraged, while neglected mosques and theological institutions were enthusiastically restored. Members of the resurgent ulema were also rewarded with increased salaries, pensions, and other allowances.

In order to maintain his influence among former Ottoman territories Abdul Hamid selected and appointed Islamic teachers to the Crimea, Cyprus, Egypt, and Bulgaria. Senior government positions were filled with Syrian and Lebanese Arabs, often in preference to Ottoman Turks, and Muslim leaders from all over the world were invited to Istanbul. Extended visits by influential Muslims such as the Indian Shia the Nawab of Oudh, and the Persian Sayyid Jemal al-din Al-Afghan, a renowned Islamic philosopher, further strengthened the sultan's role as Caliph. By the middle of his reign, despite economic problems at home, he was revered throughout the Muslim world.

Growing reverence, however, did little to stem economic decline and increasing unease at the sultan's autocratic style. As Abdul Hamid cut military expenditure and reduced the army's ability to respond to separatist uprisings, officers began to support social reforms, promulgated by the Committee of Union and Progress (CUP), and an end to political interference in military affairs. Despite being suppressed in and around Istanbul the CUP continued to gain strength. In response, the sultan became more entrenched and suspicious than ever. In the palace he strengthened the role of his secret police and continued to centralize power in his own hands, marginalizing his bureaucrats and Grand Vizier. While functionaries awaited orders, the administration almost ground to a halt.

In an attempt to steal the CUP's thunder Abdul Hamid recalled parliament on 23 July 1908, but this was not enough to enable the ageing sultan to hold on to the reins of power. Many felt that three decades of autocratic rule was enough. On 24 April 1909 troops loyal to the Young Turk revolutionaries advanced on Yildiz Palace. Initial efforts by palace troops to hold their ground melted away as guards fled the royal enclosure. General panic ensued among the servants and palace women as eunuchs spread rumours about enemy troops on the verge of entering the palace. Abdul Hamid did nothing to reassure them but shut himself away in

The mother-of-pearl dining-room in the Şale Pavilion, the only room with a distinct 'oriental' feel.

the Little Mabeyn, smoking heavily, wandering between his bedroom and living-room accompanied by his favourite son, Prince Abdurrahmin. He had neither the will nor strength left to resist the inevitable. A deputation, headed by General Essad Pasha, marched to the sultan's quarters where they calmly announced that he had been deposed on the orders of the National Assembly. It was an unspectacular ending to a long and notorious reign.

EXILE AND REVOLT

With the fall of Abdul Hamid the role of the royal harem declined; only a few favourites accompanied the sultan into exile in Salonica, where the CUP reformers had plotted their rise to power. The rest of the harem women were initially taken from Yildiz to Topkapi Palace in thirty-three carriages. But the old seraglio was in such a pitiful state of repair that they were forced to return to Yildiz while the new government arranged for their relatives to collect them. Messages were sent to Circassian villagers that their daughters and sisters, sold into the harem by their relatives or offered for the sultan's pleasure, were now free and could return to their old lives. Since leaving their native homes the harem women had obviously changed. They had clear complexions, dressed in the best materials available, and had adopted sophisticated airs, so it was difficult for many to return to the rural backgrounds which, in many ways, were as claustrophobic as the palace walls. More than half the women were 'claimed', but many of the older ones had no living relatives and others were spurned by their kinfolk.

Looters from the army which had led the coup took their revenge on sultanic privilege, destroying the imperial gold carriage, smashing gifts from foreign sovereigns, plundering a collection of mounted butterflies and stuffed birds, and stealing furniture from the ground floor of the Şale Pavilion. The rest of the furniture was distributed to other palaces, much of the court dispersed and the chief eunuch hanged from Galata Bridge; so that when Mehmet V ascended the throne in 1909 he was served by a smaller staff than his predecessors. At first Mehmet lived at Dolmabahçe, where he had resided in the princes' apartments during his brother's reign. The grand palace salons were dusted and cleaned, curtains and upholstery replaced, but with a reduced staff and imperial expenses, many rooms remained empty. The forbidding grandeur of Dolmabahçe Palace, however, soon proved too much for the sensitive Mehmet and in 1912 he moved to the intimacy of Yildiz.

Mehmet V was a good-natured but ineffective sultan whose authority was increasingly usurped by the Young Turks and their supporters. On 21 August 1909 a new law radically altered the balance of power in the CUP's favour. While the sultan retained much of his wealth, his palatial estates and private treasury, he lost control over his ministers and Grand Vizier who were now answerable to parliament. The cabinet was chosen by the Grand Vizier and each chamber elected its own president and vice-president. The sultan retained his right to choose the Sheikh-ul-Islam and the Grand Vizier, although he could only conclude treaties subject to the approval of the parliament. Even the sultan's secretary, his chief chamberlain, and their staffs were appointed by and responsible to the cabinet, thus preventing Mehmet V from building up a personal bureaucratic structure like his predecessor.

The new parliament, recalled during the last year of Abdul Hamid's reign, was initially greeted with enthusiasm and demonstrations of popular support on the streets of Istanbul. But the feeling of relief, of release from autocracy, was shortlived, giving way to disillusion and hostility between competing ideologies and antagonistic groups. Nationalist movements gained strength in the Balkans and Arab lands. European imperial powers extended their influence in the region and four major wars in less than a decade brought the empire to the verge of collapse.

Trouble began in Albania, where nationalists took to the streets to demand greater autonomy. Even though the sultan's powers had been reduced, he remained an influential figurehead and was sent to Kossovo in June 1911 in an attempt to calm the situation. In north Africa the Ottomans lost part of Libya after Italian forces landed on the African coast and annexed Tripoli and Benghazi. And in the first of two Balkan Wars, Montenegrans moved into north Albania, the Serbs seized much of northern Macedonia, Greek troops captured several Aegean islands and marched into Salonica in November 1912, just one week after Abdul Hamid had returned to Istanbul and imprisonment in Beylerbey Palace. In two months the Ottomans lost four-fifths of their territory in Europe and thousands of Balkan Turks fled to Istanbul.

Many of the failures in foreign policy leading up to the First World War were blamed on the Young Turks. The sultan tried to assert himself, speaking out against the army's involvement in politics, but his hands were tied, his voice mute. Other members of the royal family were openly hostile to the Committee of Union and Progress and, as feelings turned against the unionists, democracy degenerated into a CUP dictatorship.

Within the confines of Yildiz Palace, Mehmet turned to poetry and the company of the court. In May 1912 he employed a new governess, Safiye Ünüvar, to teach the royal children. In her reminiscences she provides one of the few first-hand accounts of life at Yildiz towards the end of the empire. It presents a contrasting picture to the turbulent world outside. As she passed through the palace gates on her first day she trembled with excitement as the carriage took her 'to another world'. Safiye was summoned before the housekeeper, 'a gentlewoman of considerable presence' who wore an ankle-length gown and short 'salta' jacket. The young teacher was asked to give religious lessons to the harem ladies in her spare time, in addition to her obligations to the princes and princesses. 'Your predecessor made some disrespectful remarks when teaching the Holy Koran and was dismissed on this account,' explained the housekeeper. 'You are the daughter of a theologian, so you will be better informed of this matter than I.'

After meeting the housekeeper Safiye was escorted to her apartments and introduced to her lady-in-waiting, three maids, a black eunuch, and a footman. During her first week palace women eagerly instructed her in the etiquette of her new surroundings. 'When I saw their exquisite manners and civility,' she wrote, 'I understood why pashas always preferred to marry women who had served at the palace.' On the first Sunday she had another room full of inquisitive visitors 'talking with pleasing Caucasian accents, hard to comprehend'.

Safiye soon had her hands full teaching the palace ladies theology, spelling, mathematics and the Koran, on top of the princes' lessons which emphasized the importance of Islam. After she had begun to adapt to palace life, Safiye was received by the sultan's wives. Although it was customary for visitors to sit on cushions, she was offered a chair, in recognition of her position as royal governess, while her lady-in-waiting sat nearby on a floor cushion. She developed close friendships with some of the wives, although one complained to her husband that Safiye was too young to teach the royal children.

However peaceful life appeared to Safiye Ünüvar, outside the walls of Yildiz the Ottoman empire was rapidly being drawn into the First World War. And it was the Turks' alliance with Germany, and their subsequent defeat by the Allies, which effectively brought to an end six centuries of Ottoman rule. The last members of the dynasty hung on for a few more years, sustained by inertia rather than a real desire to rule. Towards the end of the war Mehmet V died and was replaced by Abdul Mecit's eldest son, Mehmet VI Vahideddin, a slight old man who, as relatives' children were fond of pointing out, had the features of an owl. He inherited an empire that was in dire straits. The alliance with Germany had been a fatal mistake, leaders of the CUP, Talat, Enver, and Cemal, had fled to Germany, and by the autumn of 1919 the once proud capital was under allied occupation. Swarms of refugees strained the city's already meagre resources; Arabs, who had achieved respectable positions in Ottoman society, fled to their newly liberated homelands. In the streets people were starving, thieves thrived, and Greeks who had pledged their allegiance to the Ottoman Empire for centuries embraced foreign soldiers as their liberators.

At the Paris Peace Conference in January 1919 the victors, Britain, France, Italy, the United States, and Greece, discussed ways of dividing the remains of the Ottoman Empire between themselves and the Armenian and Kurdish minorities. Sultan Mehmet VI, who had long held sympathies with Britain and France, supported co-operation with the Allies as a means of salvaging something from the mess. Disputes among the Allies, however, delayed a final settlement until the Treaty of Sèvres, signed in August 1920. This effectively carved Anatolia into spheres of influence: the French were to get much of the south-east bordering on Syria; the British were allotted the Kurdish highlands; the Italians landed at and occupied Antalya; the Armenians were to recover ancient provinces in the east; and the Greeks were promised Izmir and its Aegean hinterland. The Turks were to get the left-overs: the poorer areas of north and central Anatolia.

The Allies' plans, however, had already been overtaken by events. In the Anatolian heartlands nationalist fervour was beginning to stir. On 19 May 1919, five days after Greek troops landed in Izmir, a brilliant young Ottoman officer, Mustafa Kemal, arrived in Samsun with plans for organizing Turkish resistance. At first Kemal was powerless to prevent the Greek advance as they quickly took control of Izmir, moving inland as far as the Menderes valley, before launching a second offensive in June 1920. Although dismissed by the sultan as a rebel, Kemal gained the support and trust of local Turkish commanders and Ankara became the centre of the nationalist struggle. By the summer of 1922 the nationalists were sufficiently organized to plan a counter-attack. In a sweeping offensive, from Izmit southwards, Greek troops were sent fleeing back to Izmir. A month later there was no effective Greek resistance left on the Anatolian mainland.

The victory ensured Kemal's undisputed leadership of the Turkish nationalists. Although many of his supporters still favoured retaining the sultanate, no one objected when Kemal called for its abolition at a meeting of the Ankara government on 31 October 1922. Sultan Mehmet VI realized that the days of the House of Osman were strictly numbered and two weeks later he fled Istanbul aboard a British destroyer, accompanied by his son, his chamberlain, several eunuchs, and some servants. He died in San Remo four years later.

PALACES OF THE PEOPLE

A porcelain stove, manufactured in the Yildiz workshops, in the selamlik entrance hall of the Şale Pavilion.

The flight of Mehmet VI effectively brought to an end the rule of the house of Osman and the ostentatious lifestyle associated with the imperial court. After his fall, Abdul Mecit II, Abdul Aziz's son, served briefly as the Caliph, the leading religious dignitary in the Islamic world, but he was no longer sultan. In a ceremony that lacked any sense of occasion or imperial splendour, Abdul Mecit was invested at Topkapi Palace by a delegation of Ankara deputies who simply informed him that he had been elected Caliph by majority vote. It was clear that the republicans attached little importance to the position and on 3 March 1924 the Grand National Assembly, following their earlier decision to abolish the sultanate, abolished the caliphate as well.

After the proclamation of the Turkish republic in 1923 the old palaces were abandoned or neglected, an unwanted symbol of the Ottoman past. Gradually, however, they were brought back into use and most are now museums. As early as the late 1920s several of the kiosks and the vast porcelain collection at Topkapi Palace were opened to the public. In suitable revolutionary rhetoric Mustafa Kemal, later to be called Atatürk, the 'father' and president of the new republic, declared that Dolmabahçe Serai was now the 'Palace of the People'. Dolmabahçe has retained its role as a centre of state protocol and is also a museum open to the public; the princes' apartments house the State Painting and Sculpture Museum. In the mind of the average Turk, Dolmabahçe Palace is linked with the memory of Atatürk, as much as the nineteenth-century sultans, for it was here that he died on 10 November 1938, soon after the fifteenth anniversary of the Turkish Republic.

Of all the ex-sultans' palaces, Yildiz Serai has witnessed the greatest number of changes since the 1920s. Some of the pavilions have served as ministerial offices, others as university buildings, while the ceremonial apartments enjoyed brief notoriety as the Casino Municipal de Yildiz, complete with bar and dance floor. Subsidiary buildings were subsequently neglected and several demolished but since the early 1980s the Yildiz complex has begun to enjoy a new lease of life.

The Turkish Touring and Automobile Association, the country's principal conservation trust, took the lead with the restoration of several pavilions, including the Malta Kiosk, in the palace's outer gardens. At the start of the decade buildings of the inner court became the headquarters of the Research Centre for Islamic History, Art, and Culture (IRCICA). Work began with the renovation of the Seyir or Observation Kiosk; the Çit Pavilion, where foreign ambassadors were once received by the sultan; and D'Aronco's *yaveran* building, where the centre's library and workshops are housed. In a little over a decade IRCICA has established itself as one of the leading Islamic arts and cultural institutes anywhere; a fitting tribute to the palace of the last great Ottoman sultan.

While Yildiz was the last of the Ottoman palaces, Topkapi Serai remains the ultimate symbol of sultanic rule and an expression of classical Ottoman culture. Seventy years after the formation of the republic many of the rooms in the labyrinthine harem are still locked awaiting restoration, their windows, perhaps, unopened since the days of Mahmut II. It was during Mahmut's reign that Julia Pardoe wrote *The Beauties of the Bosphorus* in which she sought to record the traditional customs and the settings of the city before they changed beyond recognition. Ancient customs and dress have long since disappeared, the corridors and tiled rooms of the grand seraglio peopled only by ghosts of the past, but Julia Pardoe would undoubtedly be pleased that this great oriental palace has survived largely intact. She would probably be less enamoured of the nineteenth-century

The Hamidiye fountain, complete with calligraphic panels and *Abdul Hamid's* tughra.

palaces built after her happy sojourn. But they, more than Topkapi Serai, are indicative of the city's split personality and of the direction in which Turkey has been moving for at least 150 years. More than any other art form the sultans' imperial palaces reflect the shifting cultural allegiances of a city perched on the threshold of two continents, presenting to both east and west a gateway into two merging worlds.

OTTOMAN SULTANS
(AFTER THE FALL OF CONSTANTINOPLE)

Mehmet II (the Conqueror)	1453–1481		Tiled Kiosk, 1472
Beyazit II	1481–1512	1501–1703	
Selim I	1512–1520	THE 'GOLDEN AGE'	
Süleyman the Magnificent	1520–1566	OR 'CLASSICAL	
Selim II	1566–1574	OTTOMAN STYLE'	
Murad III	1574–1595		Murad III Bedroom
Mehmet III	1595–1603		
Ahmet I	1603–1617		
Mustafa I	1617–1618		
Osman II	1618–1622		
Mustafa I (restored)	1622–1623		
Murad IV	1623–1640		Revan Kiosk, 1636
			Baghdad Kiosk, 1639
Ibrahim	1640–1648		Bower, Topkapi, 1640
Mehmet IV	1648–1687		
Süleyman II	1687–1691		
Ahmet II	1691–1695		
Mustafa II	1695–1703		Köprülü Yali, 1699
Ahmet III	1703–1730	TULIP PERIOD	Ahmet III Library,
			Fountain & Fruit Room
Mahmut I	1730–1754		Sofa Kiosk, 1752
			(refurbished)
Osman III	1754–1757	1730–1808	
Mustafa III	1757–1774	'TURKISH BAROQUE'	Sa'dullah Yali, 1760s
Abdul Hamid I	1774–1789		Sherifler Yali, 1782 (rebuilt)
Selim III	1789–1807		Aynalikavak Pavilion
			(refurbished)
Mustafa IV	1807–1808		
Mahmut II (the Reformer)	1808–1839	1808–1867	Alay Kiosk, Topkapi
		'EMPIRE'	
Abdul Mecit	1839–1861		Abdul Mecit Kiosk
			Dolmabahçe, 1856
			Beylerbey, 1865
Abdul Aziz	1861–1876	1867–1908	Çirağan, 1874
Murad V	1876	'COSMOPOLITAN'	
Abdul Hamid II	1876–1909		Yildiz Palace
Mehmet V	1909–1918	1908–1923	
Mehmet VI	1918–1922	'YOUNG TURK'	
Abdul Mecit (Caliph)	1922		

GLOSSARY

❖

bayram religious holiday or feast day, especially the festival folowing the fast of Ramadan.

bey chief of district or lower military rank.

caique light rowing-boat used on Bosphorus.

cumba any projecting part of a building including a bay window and balcony.

dervish member of a religious mystic order.

devshirme levy of boys, usually Christian, taken from conquered territories.

divan the State Council. The royal divan met in the second court at Topkapi Palace. Also a long, low seat set against a wall, particularly within a recessed bay.

fez flat-topped conical felt cap, forbidden in 1925.

firman imperial edict or permit.

gazi fighter for Islam against the infidel.

grand vizier highest rank in Ottoman empire below sultan, equivalent of prime minister.

hamam Turkish bath.

han large commercial building, also inn or caravanserai.

hanum lady.

haseki favourite wife of sultan.

iftar meal taken at sundown during the Ramadan fast.

ikbal slave girl and future concubine.

imam religious leader, head of local Muslim community.

janissary slave soldier originally conscripted from devshirme.

kanum dulcimer.

kavukluk turban holder, usually a small wooden shelf or bracket fixed to the wall.

khedive title of Ottoman governor of Egypt.

kiosk (köşk) a small pavilion, summer-house or country villa.

kismet destiny, fate or luck.

konak large town house.

mabeyn literally 'in between'; the area between the sultan's private apartments and his family (or harem), and the outer areas where the affairs of state were conducted.

mangal brazier.

medrese Muslim school.

mehtab moonlight.

mesjid small mosque.

Mevlevi member of the Whirling Dervish order.

mihrab niche in a mosque indicating the direction of Mecca.

ney flute-like instrument.

ocak fireplace with a tall, slender cap in bronze or plaster. Also a Janissary unit.

otağ or otak large nomadic tent.

pasha Ottoman title for senior political and military positions.

saz guitar-like stringed instrument.

sedir divan, sofa or raised platform.

selâmlik male section of a large Muslim house; sultan's Friday procession to the mosque.

şelsebil wall-mounted fountain with projecting 'cups'; from şelâle (waterfall) and sebil (public fountain).

serasker Ottoman Commander-in-Chief.

Sheikh-ul-Islam chief religious dignitary of the empire.

sherbet sweet summer drink.

Sherif formerly a title of the Governor of Mecca.

sofa principal hall, also sofa (seating).

tandur oven or rudimentary form of heating.

Tanzimat period of political reform during the reigns of Abdul Mecit and Abdul Aziz (1839–76).

tekke dervish lodge.

tombak copper ware.

tughra the Sultan's monogram or seal.

turbe tomb or mausoleum.

ulema leading religious functionaries, doctors of Muslim theology.

vizier highest military and administrative rank in Ottoman empire below sultan.

yashmak veil worn by Turkish women.

zeybek former soldier (orig. rebel) from the Aegean region of Turkey.

BIBLIOGRAPHY

✦

Adelsen, Charles, 'Saving Istanbul', *Architectural Review*, London, April 1978, pp. 238–46.

Akozan, Feridun, *The Sait Halim Paşa Yali*, Ankara, undated.

Atil, Esin (ed), *Turkish Art*, Smithsonian Institution, Washington, 1980.

(Author unknown), *D'Aronco Architetto*, Milan, 1982.

Barber, Noel, *The Sultans*, New York, 1973.

Berchet, Jean-Claude, *Le Voyage en Orient: Anthologie des voyageurs français dans le Levant au XIXème siècle*, Paris, 1985.

Brayer, A., *Neuf Années à Constantinople*, Paris, 1836.

Burnaby, Captain Fred, *On Horseback Through Asia Minor*, London, 1877.

Çizgen, Engin, *Photography in the Ottoman Empire, 1839–1919*, Istanbul, 1987.

Cuddon, J. A., *The Owl's Watchsong: A Study of Istanbul*, London, 1960.

Davis, Fanny, *The Ottoman Lady. A Social History from 1718–1918*, New York, 1986.

de Blowitz, Henri, 'A Trip to Constantinople – An Audience with the Sultan', *The Times*, London, 12 Nov. 1883.

Dwight, H. G., *Constantinople – Settings and Traits*, New York, 1907.

Eldem, Sedad Hakki, *Le Yali de Köçeoğlu à Bebek*, Istanbul, 1977.

—, *Reminiscences of the Bosphorus*, Istanbul, 1979.

Ertug, Ahmet, *Topkapi – The Palace of Felicity*, Istanbul, undated.

Esin, Emel, *A History of Pre-Islamic and Early Islamic Turkish Culture*, Istanbul, 1980.

—, *The Yali of Sa'dullah Pasha (An Eighteenth Century House on the Bosphorus)*, Istanbul, 1984.

Freely, John, and Sumner-Boyd, Hilary, *Strolling Through Istanbul*, Istanbul, 1972.

Garnett, Lucy M. J., *Turkish Life in Town and Country*, London, 1904.

Gebhard, David, 'Raimondo D'Aronco e l'Art Nouveau in Turchia', *Architettura, Cronache e Storia*, Dec. 1966, Jan. 1967, Feb. 1967 and March 1967.

Goodwin, Godfrey, *A History of Ottoman Architecture*, London, 1971.

Grey, The Hon. Mrs William, *Journal of a Visit to Egypt, Constantinople, Greece, &c. in the Suite of the Prince and Princess of Wales*, London, 1869.

Gülersoy, Çelik, *Dolmabahçe Palace and Its Environs*, Istanbul, 1990.

—, *Küçüksu: Meadow-Fountain-Palace*, Istanbul, 1985.

Hanum, Melek, *Thirty Years in the Harem or the Autobiography of Melek Hanum*, New York, 1872.

Herodotus, *The Histories*, Penguin Classics, 1954.

Kelly, Laurence (intro), *Istanbul: A Travellers' Companion*, London, 1987.

Le Corbusier, *Journey to the East*, Cambridge, Mass., 1987.

Lemprière, John, *Lemprière's Classical Dictionary of Proper Names Mentioned in Ancient Authors Writ Large*, London, 1788.

Levey, Michael, *The World of Ottoman Art*, London, 1975.

Llewellyn, Briony, and Newton, Charles, *The People and Palaces of Constantinople: Watercolours by Amadeo Count Preziosi 1816–1882*, London, 1985.

Loti, Pierre, *Suprêmes Visions d'Orient: Fragments de Journal Intime*, Paris, 1921.

McIlroy, A. Louise, *From a Balcony on the Bosphorus*, London, 1923.

Mansel, Philip, *Sultans in Splendour: The Last Years of the Ottoman World*, London, 1988.

Orga, Irfan, *Portrait of a Turkish Family*, London, 1950.

Osmanoglou, Aïché (Princesse Ottomane, 1887–1960), *Avec mon père le Sultan Abdulhamid de son palais à sa prison*, Paris, 1991.

Page, Bruce, Leitch, David, and Knightley, Phillip, *Philby — The Spy Who Betrayed a Generation*, London, 1968.

Pardoe, Julia, *Beauties of the Bosphorus*, London, 1839.

—, *The City of the Sultan and the Domestic Manners of the Turks in 1836*, London, 1838.

Pears, Sir Edwin, *Forty Years in Constantinople: The Recollections of Sir Edwin Pears, 1873–1915*, London, 1916.

, *Life of Abdul Hamid*, New York, 1917.

Penzer, N. M., *The Harem*, London, 1936.

Pick, Christopher (ed), *Embassy to Constantinople — The Travels of Lady Mary Wortley Montagu*, London, 1988.

Porter, Commodore D., *Constantinople and Its Environs in a Series of Letters by an American Long Resident at Constantinople*, New York, 1835.

Rice, David Talbot, *Constantinople*, London, 1965.

Saladin, H., *Le Yali des Keupruli à Anatoli Hisar Côté Asiatique du Bosphore*, Société des Amis de Stanboul, Paris, 1915.

Severin, Tim, *The Jason Voyage: The Quest for the Golden Fleece*, London, 1985.

Shaw, Stanford J., *History of the Ottoman Empire and Modern Turkey. Volume 1: Empire of the Gazis: The Rise and Decline of the Ottoman Empire, 1280–1808*, Cambridge, 1976.

Shaw, Stanford J., and Shaw, Ezel Kural, *History of the Ottoman Empire and Modern Turkey. Volume 2: Reform Revolution, and Repubic: The Rise of Modern Turkey, 1808–1975*, Cambridge, 1977.

Sherwood, John, *No Golden Journey: A Biography of James Elroy Flecker*, London, 1973.

Tugay, Emine Foat, *Three Centuries: Family Chronicles of Turkey and Egypt*, London, 1963.

Tuğlaci, Pars, *The Role of the Balian Family in Ottoman Architecture*, Istanbul, 1990.

INDEX

Abbas Hilmi II, Khedive of Egypt 90,
134, 140, **142**
Abdul Aziz, Sultan 21, 22, 79, 151,
151, 177, 182, **182**, 185, 191,
194, 195, 198–9, 201–3, 218
Abdul Hamid I, Sultan 70
Abdul Hamid II, Sultan 22, 90, 123,
129, 134, 151, 166, 172, 191,
199, 201–3, **204**, 206, 208–
10, 213–15, **218**
Abdul Mecit, Sultan **10**, 21, 22, 29,
31, 77, 79, **100**, 117, 122,
151, 154, 160, 161, **161**, 172,
177, 182, 185, 201, 216
Abdul Mecit II, Sultan 149, 218
Abdullah Pasha, Sherif of Mecca 117
Abdurrahmin, Prince 214
Afif Pasha yali **138**, **139**
Aga Hüseyin Pasha 117
Ahmet I, Sultan 154
Ahmet III, Sultan 16, 35, 40, 50, 61,
63, 64, **64**, 66, **66**, **68**, 70, **75**,
89, 146, 149
Aiwazovsky, Ivan Konstantinovich
166
Albania 35, 215
Albert, Prince 166
Alexander the Great 10
Alexander of Serbia, King 166
Alexandria 198
Alhambra, Granada 185, 191
Allom, Thomas 141
Altai Mountains 84
Anadolu Hisar ('Asian Fortress') 10,
19, **130**, **131**, **133**, **144**, 149
Anatolia 14, **159**, 160, 161, 194,
216
Ankara 26, 134, 206, 216, 218
Antalya 216
architecture and design
Armenian 21
Art Nouveau 129, 134, 141, **142**,
202
Baroque 31, 75, 79, 166
Byzantine 21, **36**
Cosmopolitan **136**, **138**, **139**
Empire **121**, 122, 194
European influence 151, 154,
160–1, 172, 194, 209
Graeco-Roman 21
Italianate 84
Iznik 21, 22
Neo-baroque 129
Neo-classicism 129
Ottoman 16, 17, 21, 22, 26, 31,
49, 51, 54, 57–8, 64, 66, 70,
79, 89, 106, 116, 117, 122–3,
129, 134, **142**, 146, 151, 154,
160, 172, 185, 191, 195
Persian 21

architecture and design (cont.)
Renaissance 22, 54, **156**, 161
Rococo 22, 64, 70, 79
Seljuk 17, 21, 106
Timurid **49**, 51
Turkish baroque 64, 70, 111,
116–17, 129, 151, 161
Uygur 84, 89
Armenian peoples 14, 17, 21, 95,
216
Arnavutköy 10, 26
Atatürk, Mustafa (Mustafa Kemal)
151, 166, 216, 218
Augusta Victoria, Empress (Germany)
206
Austria 111
Austro-Hungarian Empire 61
Ayesha, wife of Muhammad 43
Aynalikavak Pavilion 70
Composition Room **73**
Mirrored Poplar Pavilion 70
Royal Audience Chamber (Throne
Room) 70, **75**, **76**
Aynalikavak Treaty (1784) 70
Ayyubid period 123

Baffo, Safieh **52**, 57
Baghdad 40, **57**, 58, 206
Baghdad Railway 17, 27
Bali Kalfa 161
Balian, Agop 161, 194, 202
Balian family 21, 22, 75, 79, 154,
159, 160–1, **166**, **180**, 194,
202
Balian, Garabed 134, **156**, **159**, 160,
161
Balian, Nigoğos 159, 161, 166, **174**,
182, 185, 194, 202
Balian, Sarkis 161, 194, 202, 203,
206
Balian, Simon 202
Balkan Wars 129, 215
Barbarossa, Hayreddin 14, 16
Bartlett, William **100**, 141
Bastimar, Ayse 146
Battle of Bedr 43
Bebek 129, 134
Bebek Bay 90
Belgrade Forest 22
Bellini, Gentile 209
Berchère, Narcisse 123
Beşiktaş 16
Bey, Sami 90
Bey, Vedat 134
Beyazit I, Sultan **19**
Beykoz Palace 14
Beykoz ware **97**
Beylerbey Palace 21, 29, 51, 90,
185, **189**, 194–5, **196**, **197**,
201, 210, 215
Beyoğlu **134**, 160
Birgi, Muharrem Nurgi **97**

Black Sea 9, 10, 26, 28, 70, 84, 111
Blanch, Lesley 57
Blue Mosque (Sultan Ahmet Mosque)
57–8, **93**, 208
Bosnia 35
Bosphorus
crossings 10, 26, **151**
currents **4**, 10
early accounts of 9–10
embassies 22, 26
marine traffic 26, 28
waterfront 9–29, **22**
Bostancibaşi 17
Brayer, A. 17
Brighton Pavilion 22
Britain 22, 28, 50–1, 160, 198, 201,
208, 216
British community 17, 26, 95, 111,
134
Buddhism 84
Bulgaria 35, 160, 213
Burgess, Guy 95
Burnaby, Captain Fred 199
Bursa 31, 160
Büyük Mabeyn 213
Byron, Lord 9, 21, 43, 79, 141
Byzantine Empire 10, 16, 21
Byzantium see Istanbul
Bzas legend 10

Cairo 37, 40, 198
Cambon, Paul 208
Casino Municipal de Yildiz 218
Catherine the Great (Russia) 70
Çelebi, Evilya 10, 75, 154
Cemal Pasha 129, 216
Çengelköy 111
ceramics
Iznik 21, 54, 57, 58, 61, 123
Kütahya 122, **130**, 172, **173**
Seljuk 17
Çerkes Hasan 199
Charles V, Emperor 54
Çiragan Caddesi 191
Çiragan Palace 66, 122, **182**, **184**,
185, 191, **191**, 194, 198, 199,
201, 202, **204**
Çiragan Palace Hotel **19**, **184**, 194
Circassia 214
Çit Kasir 213
Clashing (Cyanean) Rocks 9, 10
Clément, Félix Auguste **131**
Committee of Union and Progress
(CUP) 123, 129, 213, 214,
215, 216
Congress of Berlin 203
Constantinople see Istanbul
Crete 160
Crimea 70, 111, 213
Crimean War (1854–6) 28, **151**,
160, 161, 177

Critoboulus **68**
Çubuklu 134, **140**, 141, **142**
Cudden, J.A. 151
Çürüksulu Ahmet Pasha yali **93**, **95**,
97
Cyprus 213

Dallam, Thomas 50–1
Daman Ibrahim Pasha, Grand Vizier
16, 66
Damascus 43
Danube, River 9
Darius 10
D'Aronco, Raimondo 129, 141, 202,
206, **206**, 210, 218
Deutsche Bank 206
Dolmabahçe Mosque 172, 210
Dolmabahçe Palace 16, 21, 22, 29,
51, 90, **134**, 151–72, 177,
182, 185, 191, 194, 195, 199,
201, 202, 206, 208, 214, 218
Ceremonial Hall (Throne Room)
156, 161, **161**, **164**, 166, 177
chandelier **161**, 166, 209
clock tower **159**
façade 151, **151**, **155**
gardens 154, **156**, **159**, 161, 177
gateways **159**, 161, **174**
Grand Staircase **164**, 166, **166**,
168
harem **173**, 177
Imperial Hamam **168**, 172
Mabeyn Salon **156**, 166
Painted Dome **161**, 166
rebuildings 154
reception rooms **169**
Sufera (ambassador's salon) **173**
Zülvecheyn room 172
Don, River 9
Donizetti, Gaetano 154
Donizetti, Giuseppe 154
Duplessis, Jean-Claude 70
Dupré, Léon 123
Dwight, H.G. 117, 213

École des Beaux-Arts 151, 161
Edirne 14, 31, 54, 61, 89, 116
Edward VII, King (Britain) 198
Edward VIII, King (Britain) 194
Egypt 40, 43, 134, 141, 198, 213
Egyptian community 17, 134
Egyptian consulate, Bebek 129, 134,
142
Egyptian villa, Çubuklu 134, **140**,
141, **142**
Eliot, Sir Charles 210
Elizabeth I, Queen (England) 50
Emirgan **112**, 117, 149
Emirğune, Prince 117
Enver Pasha 129, 216
Erivan **49**, 58, 117
Eski Serai (Old Seraglio) 14

Essad Pasha, General 214
Ethem Pertev yali, Kanlica **136**
Eugénie, Empress (France) 22, **185**, 195
European Community 29
Eyup Mosque 51

Fazil Ahmet Pasha 106, 111
Fener 122
Fenerbahçe 185
Ferdinand, Crown Prince 166
Fethi Ahmet Pasha **100**, 146, 166
Fethi Ahmet Pasha yali *see* Mocan yali
Flecker, James Elroy 95
Fontainebleau 66
France 22, 28, 160, 198, 201, 208, 216
François I, King (France) 54
Franz Joseph, Emperor (Austria) 166, 194
Fuad, King 141

Galata **31**, 50
Galata Bridge 214
Galatasaray School 54, **134**, 191
Garnett, Lucy 100
Garnier, Charles 122, 161
Gasparin, Comtesse de 26–7
Gautier, Théophile **169**
Gazi Osman Pasha, Field Marshal 203, 213
George IV, King (Britain) 22
Germany 22, 129, 206, 208, 216
Gérôme, Jean-Léon 102
Golden Horn **10**, 14, 16, **29**, **31**, 50, 54, 61, **63**, 66, 70, **75**, 89, 122, 202, **216**
Götürk Empire 84
Grand Seraglio *see* Topkapi Serai
Greece 215, 216
Greek community 14, 17, 95
Grey, Mrs William 177, 182, 195, 198
Guatelli Pasha 182
Gyllius, Petrus 10

Haedo, Abbot Diego de 16
Haghia Sophia Mosque (Church of Divine Wisdom) **10**, **93**, 160
Hagop Zarifi Pasha 203
Hamdi, Osman 209
Hamidiye Mosque 210
Hanum, Melek **90**, 100, 102, 177
Hanum, Mihri 182
Harem 27, 57
Haydarpasa Railway Station **21**, 27
Hejaz 166
Hekimbaşilarin yali, Kandilli 16, **82**
Hereke carpets **191**, 206, **210**
Hicaz Railway 208
Hisar, Abdullah Şinasi 95
Hobhouse, John Cam 43, 46
Hohenzollern 206
Hornby, Lady 160
Horta, Victor 134
Hôtel de Beauharnais, Paris 22
Huguet, Victor-Pierre 166
Hungary 111
The Hunt **131**
Hüseyin Avni, Grand Vizier 198–9

Ibrahim (the Mad), Sultan **29**, 46, 58, 61, **63**
Ilhamur Pavilion **174**, **175**, **177**, 182
Imperial Academy of Fine Arts 123, 209

Imperial Council (Divan Council) 40, 43
Imperial Porcelain Factory 209–10
Imperial School 209
Imperial Theatre 172, 177
India 43
International Straits Commission 27
Iran (Persia) 58, 79, 66, 84
Iraq 84
Islam 26, 46, **63**, 64, 66, 79, 84, 89, 213, 215, 218
  see also Muhammad, Prophet *and* Muslim community
Islamic Research Centre for History, Culture and Art (IRCICA) 202, 218
Ismail Pasha, Khedive of Egypt 166
Isparta 17
Istanbul (formerly Byzantium and Constantinople) 29, 89
  ceramics production 21
  fall of Constantinople 14, 27
  guilds 75
  inventory of Constantinople 75
  occupations 27
  sieges 10, 14, **19**
  waterfront 9–29
Istanbul Central Post Office 134
Istanbul University 14
Italy 216
Izmir 216
Izmit 216

Janissary corps 35, 51, 54, 61, 66, 106, 117
  revolts **34**, 35, 40, 75
Jason and the Argonauts legend 9–10
Jewish community 14, 17, 95
Jupiter and Juno legend 9

Ka'b ibn Zuhayr 40
Kadiköy 10
Kâğithane 89
Kandilli 16, **82**, 95, 146
Kanik, Orhan Veli 9
Kanlica **136**
Kapali Çarşi (Covered Bazaar) 14
Kara Mustafa Pasha 111
Karatodori Pasha, Alexander 203
Karlowitz Treaty (1699) 111
Keçecizade Mehmet Fuat Pasha, Grand Vizier 198
Kemal, Mustafa *see* Atatürk, Mustafa
Kibrisli Mehmet Pasha, Grand Vizier **90**, 177
Kibrisli yali, Kandilli **85**, **89**, **90**, 102, 146
Kirghiz 84
Kislar Aga, Chief Black Eunuch **42**, 43
Kiz Kulesi (Maiden's Tower/ Leander's Tower) 27
Klipstein, Auguste 146
Koç yali **144**, **145**, **146**, **148**
Koca Kasim Aga 58, **61**
Konya 106
Köprülü Armcazâde Husey Pasha 111
Köprülü Armcazâde Husey Pasha yali 22, **82**, 90, 102, 106, 111, 116, 117, 134, **140**, **141**, 149
Köprülü dynasty 106
Köprülü, Fazil Mustafa Pasha 111
Köprülü Hüseyin Pasha 111
Köprülü Hüseyin Pasha yali 111, 146
Köprülü, Mehmet Pasha (Mehmet the Cruel) 106

Kossovo 215
Küçük Çelebizâde Asim Efendi 95
Küçük Kaynarca Treaty (1774) 111
Küçüksu Palace 95, **174**, **178**, **180**, 182, 185, **185**, 194
Kuleli Officers' Training College **10**, **14**
Kurdish peoples 216
Kütahya 21, **105**, 106, 122, **130**, 172, **173**
Kuzguncuk 100, **100**, 146, 191

Lamartine, Alphonse de 9
Latard, Lady 208
Le Corbusier **79**, **93**, 146
Le Roi, Gustave 206
Lemprière, John 10
Leroy, Paul 123
Levant Company 50
Libya 215
Logothetes, Nikolaos Aristarhos 122
Loti, Pierre 9, 22, **79**, 95, 146, 149
Louis XIV, King (France) 21
Louis XV, King (France) 21, **69**, 70
Louis XVI, King (France) **97**, 117, 122, 123, **133**
Lowther, Lady 149

Macedonia 215
Mahmut I, Sultan 66, 70, 182
Mahmut II, Sultan 26, 40, 43, 75, **85**, 146, 151, 154, 177, 218
Makook III 134
Mandrocles 10
Marmara Islands 26
Marmara Sea 14, 17, 26, 54, 57, 66, 84
Marshal of the In Between 198
Master of the Virgins 46
Mecca 43, **55**, 213
Mecidiye Mosque 191
Medina 213
Megarian communities 10
Mehmet II (the Conqueror), Sultan 10, 14, **19**, 31, 35, 43, 46, 51, 54, 58, 151, 209
Mehmet III, Sultan 50, 51, **52**
Mehmet IV, Sultan 34, 61, 75, 154
Mehmet V, Sultan 172, 214, 216
Mehmet VI Vahideddin, Sultan 216, 218
Mehmet Emin Ali Pasha, Grand Vizier 198
Mehmet Rüştü Pasha, Grand Vizier 198
Melling, Anton Ignaz 141, 154
Mevlevi dervishes 111, 191
Michelangelo 21
Midhat Pasha 203
Military Academy 199
Mocan yali, Kuzguncuk 95, 100, **100**, **102**, 105, 146
Mongolia 84
Montagu, Lady Mary Wortley 9, 185
Montenegro 215
Montreux Convention (1936) 28, 29
Mosque of the Barber, Kairouan 43
Mu'awiweh I 40
Muhammad Ali 134
Muhammad, Prophet 46, 89
  sacred relics 31, **37**, 40, 43
Murad III, Sultan **52**, 57, 58
Murad IV, Sultan 58, 75, 117
Murad V, Sultan 116, 191, 194, 199, 203, **204**
Muslim community 14

Mustafa III, Sultan 111
Mustafa, son of Süleyman 46

Naci, Halid 209
Nadir, Asil 111
Nadir, Ayşegül 111
Napoleon III, Emperor (France) 195, 198
Nash, John 22
Nasireddin, Shah 194
National Assembly 214
National Exhibition Centre, Istanbul 202
Nazine Sultan Palace, Ortaköy 129
Nebioğlu, Ruya 146
Necib, Altunizâde **134**
Nedim, Ahmet 66, 89–90
Netherlands 111
Nicholas II, Tsar 166
'Night of Power' 57
Nightingale, Florence 27

Old Seraglio 46
Orga, Irfan **10**
Orient Express 27, 134
Ortaköy 122, 129
Osman II, Sultan 50, 154
Osman III, Sultan **69**, 70
Osman dynasty 216, 218
Ostrorog, Count **79**, 149
Ottoman Empire 10, 14, 16, 21, 22, 28, 35, 40, 43, 46, **46**, **49**, 50, **52**, 54, 61, **82**, 89, 111, 122, 209
  architecture and decoration 16, 17, 21, 22, 26, 31, 51, 54, 57–8, 66, 70, 79, 89, 106, 117, 122–3, 129, 134, **142**, 146, 151, 154, 160, 172, 185, 191, 195
  army 35, 40, 111, 141, 198, 213
  decline 95, 111, 141, 149, 195, 198, 201, 215–16, 218
  gardens 17
  literature and theatre 66, 160
  navy 14, 16, 111, 116, 198, 202
  Westernization 151, 154, 160–1, 166, 172, 177, 206, 208, 216
Ottoman-Greek War (1897) 172
'Ottoman Rose' paint **79**, **82**, 95

Palace Theatre 202
Palladio 54
Pardoe, Julia 17, **93**, 146, 194, 218
Paris Opera House 122, 161, 172, 202
Paris Peace Conference (1919) 216
Pélissier, Maréchal 161
Pera **31**, 50
Persia *see* Iran
Pescator 26
Philby, Kim 90, 95
Plevna, Siege of 203
Pontus kingdom 14
Préault, Auguste 182
Princes' Islands 84
Princes Zeyneb's yali, Bebek 122
Puch, D. 123

Redcliffe, Lord Stratford de 161
Rhodes 160
Ricci, Luigi 177
Riza, Hoca Ali 210
Riza Pasha 177
Robilant, Comtesse de 149
Rocholi, Rudolf Theodor 166

Romania 160
Rossi, Ernesto 208
Rouillard, P. **189**
Roxelana (Haseki Hurrem) 46
Rumeli 160
Rumeli Hisar (formerly Boğaz-kesen)
  ('European Fortress') 10, 14,
  19, 185
Russia 26, 28, 61, 70, 111, 160,
  194, 203

Sa'dabat Palace ('Place of Happiness')
  16, 66, **216**
Sa'dullah Pasha, Necibe 117
Sa'dullah Pasha, Rami 116–17
Sa'dullah Pasha yali, Yeniköy **106**,
  109, **110**, 111, 116, 117, 122,
  123, 129
Sait Halim Pasha 90, 122, 123, **124**,
  129, **131**, 149
Sait Halim Pasha yali, Yeniköy **117**,
  121, 122, **122**, 123, **124**, **125**,
  126, **128**, 130, 131, 133, 134,
  208
Salacak Palace **93**
Salman 43
Salonica 208, 214, 215
Samos 160
Samsun 216
Sarayburnu ('Seraglio Point') **19**
Sayyid Jemal al-din Al-Afghan 213
Scutari Barracks 27
Séchan, M. 172
Selim I, Sultan ('the Grim') 37, 40,
  43, 54, 198
Selim II, Sultan ('the Sot') 46
Selim III, Sultan 28, 70, **73**, 75, **75**,
  77, **97**, 117, 141, 154, **204**
Seljuk peoples 17, 21, 89, 106
Seminati, Delfo **142**
Seraglio Point 10, **10**, 46, 51
Şerifler yali, Emirgan **112**, **113**, **114**,
  115, 117, 149
Severin, Tim 10
Shamanism 84
Sheikh-ul-Islam 61, 177, 203, 214
Shia the Nawab of Oudh 213
Simpson, Mrs 194
Sinan, Mimar 21, **49**, 54, 57, 58,
  160–1, 172
Sinan Pasha Mosque 172
Sirkeci Station 134
Şirket-i Hayriye 26
Slav community 14
Smyrna 208
Societé des Amis de Stamboul 149
Stampa 160
State Painting and Sculpture Museum
  166, 218
Stratford, Lord and Lady 160
Stravolo, Arturo 208

Suavi, Ali 191, 203
Sublime Porte 50, 75, **79**, 95, 111,
  149, 198
Suez Canal 195
Süleyman I, Sultan (the Magnificent)
  10, 14, 16, **22**, 46, 54, 57, 61
Süleyman II, Sultan 61
Süleyman Pasha 199
Süleymaniye Camii Mosque complex
  22, 54, 61, 210
Sultane Valide **40**, 46, 57, 195
'Sweet Waters of Asia' **178**, 182
'Sweet Waters of Europe' 16, 66
Syria 40, 208, 216

Talat Pasha 129, 216
Tanzimat Period 198, 213
Tarabya 122, 141
Tersane ('Dockyard') Palace 70, **75**
Thackeray, William Makepeace 57
Thouvenel, M. 161
Thracian community 10
Topal Mehmet Pasha 106
Topkapi Point 14, 31, 58, 77, 151
Topkapi Serai ('Cannon Gate Palace',
  Grand Seraglio) 10, 14, 21, **29**,
  31–77, 89, **93**, 116, 117, 141,
  151, 154, 160, 172, 177, 198,
  200, 202, 206, 214, 218–19
  Abdul Hamid I's Chamber 70
  Abdul Mecit's Kiosk 31, 77
  Ahmed III's Fruit Room 64, **64**,
    66, 185
  Ahmet III's Library 40, **63**, 64,
    68, 146
  Alay Kiosk **34**, 75, 77
  Baghdad Pavilion 50, **57**, 58, **58**,
    61, **61**, 64, 89
  Black Eunuch's Courtyard and
    Quarters 40, **42**, **44**
  Circumcision Room (Sünnet
    Odasi) 61
  Council Chamber 40
  Courtyard of the Cage **46**
  Courtyard of the Janissaries 35, 40
  Courtyard of the Sultane Valide **40**
  courtyards 31, 35, 40, 43, 46, **49**,
    50, 58, **63**, 64
  Divan Court **32**
  Divan Tower **33**
  fountains 43, 50, 57, **63**, 64, 66,
    68
  gardens 17, 50, **63**, 64
  Gate of Felicity (Gate of the White
    Eunuchs) **34**, 40, 43
  Gate of Offerings 43
  Gate of Salutations (Middle Gate)
    32, 40, 116
  Hall of the Pantry **36**
  harem **10**, **31**, 46, 50, 61
  Iftar Kiosk (Gilded Bower) **63**

Topkapi Serai (*cont.*)
  Imperial Gate (Gate of Perpetual
    Delight) 31, 64, **68**
  Imperial Hall (Royal Salon) **70**
  Imperial Mint 35
  Inner Palace 40
  Inner Treasury 40
  kitchens **49**, 54, 57
  Mahmut I's Kiosk 70
  Mihrisah Sultane Valide's Hall 70
  Murad III's Bedroom **52**, 57, 58
  Office of the Grand Vizier 40
  Osman III's Kiosk **69**, 70
  Outer Treasury 35
  Palace School 35, 40, **68**
  Pavilion of the Holy Mantle
    (Hirkei Şerif Odasi) **37**, 40, 50,
    202
  Prison of the Princes ('Cage') **45**,
    46, 50
  Prophet Muhammad's relics *see*
    Muhammad, Prophet
  Public Relations Office 40
  Revan Pavilion (Turban Room)
    49, 50, 58, 61, 64
  selamlik **10**, **31**, 40
  Selim III's Salon 70, 75, 77
  Sofa Kiosk **69**, 70
  Sepetciler Kiosk **28**, 61
  Sultane Valide's Apartment **9**, **38**,
    55
  Sultan's Way 40
  Throne Room 43
  Tiled Pavilion (Çinili Kiosk) 31,
    49, 51, 54, 64, 89, 161, 185
Topkapi Point 14, 31, 58, 77, 151
Tournefort, Joseph Pitton de 35
Trabzon 106
'The Trained Victorious Soldiers of
  Muhammad' 117
Transoxiana territories 84
Transylvania 111
Treaty of Paris (1856) 27
Treaty of Sèvres (1920) 216
Treaty of Unkiar Skelesi 194
Trebizond 14
Tugay, Emine Foat 90, 122
Tuileries Palace, Paris 195
Tulip Period 16, 17, 31, 61, **63**, 64,
  64, 66, 89, 90, 102, 122–3,
  149, 154, 185
Tunisia 43
Turco-Austrian Karlowitz Treaty
  (1699) **82**
Turco-Russian War (1877–8) 201
Turkish Touring and Automobile
  Club 141, 218

Ummajid dynasty 40
Unité D'Habitation, Marseilles **79**
United States of America 216

Ünüvar, Safiye 215–16
Üsküdar **93**
Uygur people and architecture 84,
  89

Valeri, Salvaro 123, 209
Vandeuvre, Monsieur **134**
Vehbi, Seyyid 66
Versailles 66, 172
'The Verse of the Throne' 57, 58
Victoria, Queen **100**, **161**, 166, 209
Vienna 61, 111, 117
Vienna Secession 129
Villeneuve, Marquis de 66

Wangenheim, Baron 129
White Sea 10
Wilhelm II, Kaiser 22, 191, **201**,
  206, 208, **210**
World Exhibition 198
World War I 28, 122, 129, 134,
  149, 215, 216

Yali Kiosk 54
yalis 79–150, **82**
Yeni Valide Mosque 57
Yeniköy 26, 90, 122, 123, 129,
  137, **138**, **139**, 208
Yenisei River 84
Yildiz Park 191
Yildiz Serai ('Palace of the Stars') 22,
  134, 151, 191, 201–16, 218
  Armoury **207**
  Çadir Pavilion 203
  Ceremonial Apartments 208
  Çit Pavilion 218
  gardens **204**, 206, **206**
  harem 214
  Hamidiye fountain **220**
  Imperial Mebeyn 203
  Little Mabeyn 214
  Malta Pavilion 203, **204**, 218
  Mother-of-Pearl Room **216**
  photographic library 209, 210
  Reception Hall 206
  Şale Pavilion 22, **201**, 206, 208,
    210, **213**, 214, **218**
  Seyir (Observation) Kiosk 218
  Yellow Room **216**
Yildiz Theatre 208
Yirmisekiz Çelebi Mehmet Efendi 66
Young Turks Revolution (1908) 123,
  129, 149, 172, 213, 214, 215

Zarif Mustafa Pasha yali **4**, **85**
Zarzecki, Warinia 123
Zeyneb, Princess 122
Zonaro, Fausto 166, 172, 208, 209,
  210